CONTENTS

———————————— *Continued on next page* ————————————

Continued from previous page

NOTES ON CONTRIBUTORS

Costis Hadjimichalis is a Greek planner, teaching at the Aristotle University, Thessalonika

Miriam Glucksmann is Professor of Sociology at Essex University

David Gibson is a freelance photographer and former residental social worker

Joanne Barkan is a New York-based writer, author of *Visions of Emancipation: The Italian Workers' Movement Since 1945*, and a member of the editorial board of *Dissent.*

Joanna Moncrieff is a Psychiatric Research Fellow at the Institute of Psychiatry, London

Phil Cohen is Director of the Centre for New Ethnicities Research at the University of East London, and author of *Rethinking the Youth Question* (1997)

Catherine Smith is currently doing an MA in Creative Writing

Ruth Valentine has published three collections of poetry: *The Identification of the Species*, *The Lover in Time of War*, and *Poems in Cathar Country.*

Judy Gahagan is author of a volume of short stories, *Did Gustav Mahler Ski?*, and two pamphlets of poetry.

Peter Porter is author of *Millenial Fables* (1994) and *Dragons in Their Pleasant Places* (1997)

Alan Woodley is Senior Research Fellow at the Institute of Education and Technology at the Open University

Ken Worpole is a freelance writer and researcher, author of *Staying Close to the River (L&W 1996)*

Christine Alhadeff is a trainee child psychotherapist at the Tavistock Clinic

James Souter tutors in Continuing Education

Sandra Bewick lives and works as a researcher in Leeds

Elizabeth Julian works in London as a freelance journalist

Kevin Davey is a marketing consultant and journalist, and author of *English Imaginaries* (L&W forthcoming)

Jonathan Rutherford is a Lecturer in Cultural Studies at Middlesex University

Jonathan Keane is a freelance journalist and broadcaster

Bilkis Malek is researching South Asian film\video cultures at Middlesex University and the British Film Institute.

continued overleaf

Elaine Pennicott is a PHD student at
Middlesex University

Ian Brinkley is a TUC researcher

John Healey was TUC Campaigns
Director until the election, and is now
Labour MP for Wentworth, South
Yorkshire

Frances O'Grady is the director of the
TUC's New Unionism Campaign

Rupa Huq is a PHD student at the
University of East London

Michael Kenny is Lecturer in Politics at
Sheffield University, currently a visiting
lecturer at William and Mary College,
USA

Peter Gartside is a freelance writer.

The morning after

It was great that night of May 1st. Labour Day.

Perhaps the most disorienting thing - the feeling most difficult to come to grips with - on that May Day Bank Holiday weekend after the election was that everything had changed and yet so little had been challenged. Not only the political but also the emotional landscape had been utterly transformed. Not only the Tories routed even in the most unexpected areas (Hove?! St Albans?!), but also a feeling of shared exhilaration - amongst friends, with the endless re-telling of the moment of Portillo's defeat, and more widely outside on the streets too. *The Guardian* captured it beautifully : 'yesterday the population went wild, British style. People were seen breaking into half-smiles in public while reading the papers; some thought about making eye contact in the Tube [regrettable London bias here]; others even considered talking to complete strangers, then remembered themselves and drew back' (Matthew Engel, 3 May 1997). Like many others who shared these feelings of uninhibited delight, this journal has had its debates with, and serious criticisms of, the project of 'New Labour'. Yet there was no disguising the joy which the victory, and the scale of the victory, awoke.

And yet of course so little change had in reality been promised. *The Guardian* also argued that 'an 18-year long Conservative experiment with the nature of Britain and the British people was obliterated' (editorial, 3 May). That is not so. Much of the fruits of that experiment both remain in place and will not be challenged. The nature of British society and of British political debate has been reworked by Thatcherism and there is no going back. Many of the institutional changes she and her successor initiated will perforce have to remain in place - they are either irreversible or too costly at this point to reverse. And much of what in the early years of Tory rule seemed revolutionary has now been accepted by New Labour as common sense. So, no, the experiment has by no means been obliterated and much of it indeed seems set to stay around for some time yet.

So what was it, that May Day weekend, that felt, and made us feel, so very different? First, it was simply the fact that the Tories were gone. All the electoral analysis makes clear this was (as well as anything else) a vote *against* the Conservatives. The high degree of tactical voting and the variations in levels of turn-out are clear evidence of that. But - second - that was itself not just a negative thing. The vote against the Tories was not the result only of the fact of their endless internal divisions and squabbles, nor of the daily, degrading, evidence of their incompetence and corruption. Those things were undoubtedly important, and indeed themselves point to a desire for a basic minimum of decency and order on the part of the electorate. But it was also more than that. The scale of the vote, and the precision of its rejection of the Tories, pointed to a degree of disenchantment and unease with the direction of the Majorite project which was spread even more widely and deeply than we had suspected.

Reworking common sense

We wrote of this disenchantment in our last editorial. On the one hand there is the unease which touches personal lives: the insecurities which result from casualisation and 'flexibility', and from creeping privatisation of the welfare state. On the other hand there is the unease which is born of (the remnants of) a wider sensibility : that there *must* be such a thing as society and we must work out what it might be; that not every nook and cranny of life should be subject to market calculation; that the new levels of inequality and unfairness have reached the intolerable; that we are doing irreparable damage to the environment and we must - somehow - stop, or at least slow down, and ponder what might be changed. In March we argued that the task of politicians (and others too, but we are concentrating on politicians here) is actively to create political subjects and political constituencies. Not only to ask people, or focus groups, what they feel/think/want *now*, but to touch those nerves, those maybe-still-barely-recognised feelings that can be the fountainhead for change. Mrs Thatcher did that. And, we argued, New Labour should far more actively have done it too. There was abroad, we argued, a kind of unease which cried out for turning into a force for progressive change.

The election results reinforce this argument in spades. The depth of the disenchantment was shown to be deep, widespread, and determined. That reinforces our argument that a project of political creation/conversion should have been begun some years ago (for these things take time).

But there is no point in talking about what might have been. The nature of the election result means surely that it can be attempted now, and with some confidence. In the last editorial we pointed to a number of areas ripe for such reworking : where the terms of debate need to be redefined; where a new political lexicon needs devising. Some will anyway force themselves on to the agenda (the nature of what we mean by the social; the need to replace the purely economic calculus of standard of living with a wider notion of the quality of life). Others need to be addressed by any government which takes seriously a mandate to be even minimally 'progressive' (internationalism comes immediately to mind - and Robin Cook's moves in that direction have already been exhilarating). What we need is a shifting of whole areas of what has come to be seen as common sense. (For, as we said earlier, it is only relatively recently that so much of our present common sense has acquired that seemingly unshiftable status.) This is a medium-term project. (It doesn't even necessarily imply any immediate spending commitments! - we say that not because we are against such commitments but because suggesting them is a guaranteed way to get yourself ignored - another bit of 'common sense' that will, eventually, have to go.)

What had changed that May Day weekend was the atmosphere. There was the relief of 'their' departure; but there was also a desire to balance (at least and already) the priorities of the past with new emphases and responsibilities; there was a sense of possibility. There was a feeling (if not an expectation) that the parameters of political discourse might shift. The very scale of the victory itself released a sense of excitement and thereby - surely - enhanced the potential for change. There was space to open up, and to begin rethinking, reconstructing, the collective imaginary.

Imagining 'the nation'

In a tentative way, one element of this imagination has already been shifted by the radical change in the composition of Parliament itself. Election night will also stay in the memory because of the fall of so many men-in-suits, to be replaced by cheery, smiling women. The representation of ethnic minorities is still pathetically low, but nonetheless a Muslim in Glasgow must present a challenge to thinking nationalism. There will be a woman in a wheelchair, a single mother, another out gay guy. The 'sense' of the nation, and of who has a right to represent it, has shifted remarkably.

Most of this change has come about through Labour's new intake. In a very palpable way the Conservatives on one side, and Labour and Liberals on the other, represent two different versions of what constitutes the United Kingdom.

It is mirrored in the very geography of their votes. It is in fact *not* simply true (as has often been asserted) that the Tories have been reduced to the shires. In terms of the votes of individuals, we have to remember that they still won between a quarter and a third of the votes in most cities. But in terms of Conservative hegemony over local culture and politics, the shires are indeed now their only domain. The expulsion of their MPs from Scotland, Wales and the major English cities has continued (where that was possible : there weren't any of them in some northern cities anyway). But with the reorganisation of constituencies they have now lost also in the smaller towns of the south east (Hatfield, Bedford, Milton Keynes, Harlow, Watford, Stevenage, Luton, Crawley, Hemel Hempstead...) ... such towns are now Labour, set in a sea of blue. The contrast between urban and rural in these parts is glaring.

It is a geographical irony. The Conservatives have had a much clearer view of 'the nation' than have Labour. They have frequently given voice to it - one of the latest versions being John Major's manufactured nostalgia for a village he never knew : warm beer, spinsters (why spinsters?) riding home on bicycles, and cricket on the village green. It is, of course, a concoction of images which only takes on, even approximately, material form in rural areas, and those mainly in the south. It has nothing to do with the windswept moors of north and west, nor with the windswept estates of big cities. Yet it was the Tories who spoke most of the nation and of the need for its continued (geographical) unity. The fact that they did it through mobilising an image which pictured only a small part of the country never seemed to bother them. And indeed for a long time it worked. It is to this small part of the country that they have now - in terms of representation - been reduced.

Labour, too, of course, in this election spoke much of 'One Nation'. They need now to come to grips with what they mean by it. Socially and geographically their votes bring together the vast array of differences which make up this country. A rhetoric of one-ness will not cover over the differences and conflicts within it. Constitutionally there are the issues of Scotland and Wales - devolution and new assemblies could be (as could Europe) good exercises in how to think relatedness and difference together. But other divisions will be far tougher to address. The Tories left the people of this country far more polarised in economic terms, for instance, than twenty years ago. It was perhaps (though we doubted it) necessary to construct a notion of one-ness in order, initially, to overcome this and, simply, to win the election. New Labour in this campaign spoke often of how it would never fall prey to the demands of sectional interests (and even while the sectional interests of the City and of business were being lavishly appealed-to, there was always the possibility that all this was necessary as a precondition for doing other things : one bit one's lip).

But it is different now; victory is secured. And the complexity, difference and inequality which makes up the nation(s) of the UK must now finally be addressed. When Tony Blair arrived at Downing Street on 2 May and was greeted by all that unalloyed enthusiasm, the crowd was waving the Union Flag. Actually it was waving hundreds of them, provided I believe by HQ. It gave pause for thought (rather than simple rejection). It can be a strong and inventive strategy to take over the enemies' symbols and icons. And the Tories have surely tried to make the flag their own in recent years. But one doesn't just take over symbols; they have to be re-worked. The strategy really does have to be one of invention too. The Union Flag needs re-signifying if it is to be used by Labour - can it be made to stand for the differences within? and for less imperialist relations without? can there, for instance, be black in the Union Jack? Labour - and we - need to define this 'new' nation.

One hint of the exclusions already implicit in this notion of one nation was already discernible from the election figures. Mixed-in with jubilation at the 'landslide' must also be sober reflection on some of the numbers. First, in absolute terms Labour's landslide was achieved with half a million fewer votes than John Major garnered in 1992. Tactical voting and first-past-the-post mean that some of Labour's support will be showing up as Liberal votes. But nonetheless ... Second, turnout was down on 1992, and indeed at 71.3 per cent was exceptionally low - the lowest since 1935. This speaks more of an increasing alienation from politics than of wild enthusiasm in all corners of the land. And third - and perhaps the most important point - the different corners of the land indeed turned out in very different numbers. My rough-and-ready analysis says clearly that turnout was lowest in (some) Labour heartlands and, especially, in inner cities. In some inner-city constituencies it sank well down into the fifties. 52.5 per cent in Manchester Central, 51.9 per cent in Liverpool Riverside, the mid-fifties from Glasgow Kelvin and Shettleston, and in Birmingham Ladywood. Now there may be many reasons for this. Maybe such areas always have turnouts lower than the national average. The impetus to vote must be less when Labour's majority is huge and assured (indeed for me one of the emotions always provoked as the results come in is wonder at the sheer dogged persistence of the millions who turn out, election after election, to do the same thing: Knowsley South: majority 31,000; Easington: majority 30,000). Moreover, the picture is not a simple one : the turnouts in Blaenau Gwent (maj : 28,000), Rhondda (25,000), Sedgefield (25,000) and Torfaen (25,000) were all *above* the national average.

But, even allowing for all these qualifications and caveats, the low turnout in certain inner-city areas in particular must give pause for thought. How are the concerns of these places to be woven into the new Labour Union Flag?

Life beyond the parties

Indeed, how are the concerns of such places to make themselves felt? Tony Blair's acceptance of much of the rhetoric of individualism means that - certainly up to the election - he seemed to view collective identifications with suspicion. It may be, again with hope, that he viewed them only as an *electoral* liability, in which case doors may be more open now. If they are not, if collectivities continue to be regarded as an alien form, then it will be most likely be as a result of their association with 'old Labour'.

As we have argued before, one of the pieces of Blair's imaginary which must most urgently be jettisoned is that all-too-easy, inaccurate, and harmful distinction between old Labour and new. It is a binary polarisation into which many of us anyway do not fit. Its mobilisation in debate is a gesture which serves to delegitimise but not to answer any arguments. It closes down thought. (And anyway, as all social theorists know, binary thinking is definitely out these days!)

But, seriously, how will voices make themselves heard to this new administration? Where are the popular roots of Blairism? Or, more significantly now, beyond the election and the votes of individuals, how will they make themselves felt? That arena of collectivities and movements, between state and individual, is attenuated now. During the election campaign the green movement made the news, and there was the fuss about Swampy; there was the churches' call for more attention to issues of inequality and redistribution; but not much more. It was a great disappointment, for instance, that the One World coalition, which attracted some attention a year ago, failed to make any impact at all. The silence indicated in some areas by a turnout of not much over fifty per cent must not remain a silence now that the election is done.

Indeed, the raising of voices and the mobilisation of social forces beyond the parties can be important to the government itself. It can demonstrate support for even minimally radical measures which dare to go beyond the establishment's interests (or even - dare to think the unthinkable - against them). Bill Clinton's attempt at health reform in the US found itself isolated and beleaguered precisely because of the lack of such forces. What appears to have been substantial grass-roots support for the policy had no means of making itself heard above the bellowing and fury of the medical-industry lobbies. In the UK, such 'fury' (in a typical headline - 'fury at government's attempt to...') might well be orchestrated by tabloid newspapers. In its editorial immediately after the election, and in an attempt to nudge the new government into a greater degree of radicalism, *The Observer* wrote that 'Labour should have wised up after the campaign; hysteria from its political opponents does not mean either that they are right or that they command widespread support. It needs to remember and succour the 62 per cent that voted for change'. Quite so. But the very fact that we were surprised at the size of that percentage, and at its canniness in voting tactics, is precisely an indication of its lack of voice outside of the polling booth. How, *between elections*, is this pressure for change going to make itself heard?

In the editorial of the very first issue of *Soundings* we spoke of the need for a wider conception of politics. That there must be a 'politics-beyond-politics'. That there is more to radicalism than what is accomplished by governments. That political actors, narrowly defined, are normally carried along by these wider currents. New left politics, anyway, must not be confined by being constructed only in relation to formal parties. What develops outside of Parliament will be at least as important, over the next five years and hopefully more, as what goes on within.

DM

What kind of Europe?

A view from the periphery

Costis Hadjimichalis

Eastern Europe and the Southern Mediterranean are emerging today as preferential partners of the EU. Official rhetoric, however, tries to mask the simultaneous processes of marginalisation and exclusion of these 'other' places, which also involve some of the less developed EU regions.

The cold war equilibrium and the Mediterranean border used to hold everything in place. There were familiar environments - and comfortable ones for those fortunate enough to live in the west. The contours were clear, the habits predictable. Today this clear picture is broken and Eastern Europeans, Oriental people, and neighbours across the sea demand their rights of entry into the Single European Space. In earlier centuries, as Braudel teaches us, they were part of it; they have contributed to its wealth and culture; they were once 'inside', and they cannot accept some of the current European notions which portray Europe's lines of inclusion/exclusion as outcomes of new global relations.

What are these relations? For many, including the European Union, this is unproblematic. They assume that the EU has 'erased all internal boundaries', and propose today to some of its neighbours in the East, and across the Mediterranean, 'equal' economic relations based on competition. Equality, however, does not exist around the Mediterranean, beyond the Elbe or the Danube - nor of course globally. The EU stands today as a powerful economic giant, with the countries and people to the East and South of it as 'poor relations'. As we come to the end of the twentieth century, the sense that we all live in 'one world' has never been stronger; but it is a deeply divided world and at the same time highly interconnected: 'their struggle' is related to 'our comfort', the 'We' constructs the 'Other'.

Bearing all this in mind, in this short essay I should like to discuss some of the EU's intentions towards Eastern Europe and the Mediterranean as they appear in official documents, trying at the same time to draw a different picture from the one which the EU promotes. In particular, I will argue that closer economic relations of these countries with the EU, without traditional protection, may work in the interest of the most powerful north-central regions and sectors of the EU, and this may further jeopardise the competitiveness of the less powerful ones, which happen to be in the south. In addition I want to focus some attention on a less discussed aspect of integration and international relations, the constructed meanings and ideas that exist about places and people, about 'insiders' and 'outsiders'. My argument is that current processes of selective inclusion/exclusion in the New Europe are founded - in addition to economic and political factors - on the old arsenal of perceptions which north-central Europeans have for those with the smell and feel of 'otherness'. These perceptions are based in turn on the supposed cultural and religious superiority of north-central Europeans - two taboo subjects which seem to play at present an increasingly active role in the hidden agenda of European integration.

Intentions and contradictions

For various reasons, the EU during the last five years has paid particular attention to Central-Eastern European Countries (CECs) and to Mediterranean countries which are not Community members (MNCs). In the East, the EU intends to include Albania, Bulgaria, Romania, Slovenia, Croatia, Hungary, the Czech and Slovak republics, Poland and the Baltic republics. In the Mediterranean the intention is to include Morocco, Algeria, Tunisia, Egypt, Lebanon, Israel and Turkey. Note that Bosnia, Yugoslavia and Russia are not included, nor Libya and Syria, while Malta and Cyprus are half-way to full membership in the EU.

The process of reform and the opening up of markets in the East, and population explosion in the Southern Mediterranean, in combination with rich energy and agricultural resources, present both opportunities and challenges for the Community. In a communication presented in October 1994, the Commission recalled the social, political and economic interconnections between the EU and the countries of the eastern and southern Mediterranean, and proposed the establishment of a Euro-Mediterranean partnership likely to lead, in due course, to the creation of a free trade area. A few years before the Commission presented a similar statement for CECs, although using a slightly different language - 'helping the transition from centrally planned to market economies', 'political stabilisation', 'environmental protection' and 'regional co-operation'. To facilitate these intentions two major programmes have been launched: PHARE and INTERREG.

'North-central Europeans draw on an arsenal of perceptions for those with the smell and feel of "otherness"'

The fall of the Berlin Wall in 1989, and the triumph of western market capitalism over eastern state pseudo-socialism, were celebrated by many in Europe, as was Europe's dissociation from US and Soviet domination. Seven years later, however, many hopes from that historical time have proven to be false ones. Europe, incapable of understanding, acting in and solving the Bosnia siuation, was forced to accept the Dayton agreement, which placed the USA again at the centre of European affairs and confirmed its dominant position. And the triumph of western capitalism over eastern states appears to have been simply a destruction of what existed before, with little hope of recovery. At present, all eastern countries are suffering deep economic recession, with high inflation, unemployment and declining real incomes, plus rising crime and Mafia-type activities. Signs of improvement are rare - with the exception of the Czech Republic - and greater job losses and increased social unrest are predicted. At the same time, however, trade relations among EU member states and regions and CECs have grown substantially, especially exports to the EU from these countries. These are composed predominantly of raw materials and basic products, including such sensitive goods as steel and textiles.

The growth of trade has been accompanied by growth of direct investment from the EU, though this remains small in most places, totalling 7.3 billion ECUs in the period 1989 to 1991, equivalent to under 10 per cent of Community direct investment to third countries. The USA and Japan have been more 'generous', investing during the same period more than 12 billion ECUs. Inflows of capital have gone disproportionately to the Czech Republic and Hungary, where the risks are lowest, and in other countries they have gone predominantly to national capitals and other major cities where job and real income losses have been least. Both trends reinforce the tendency towards uneven spatial development .

The growth of markets in Central and Eastern Europe will tend to benefit EU regions which are already competitive, and which are already strongly engaged in international trade, especially regions which, because of their location, have relatively easy access to these eastern markets. German, Austrian and Dutch regions will be the main beneficiaries, followed by Danish and Swedish regions. On the other hand, the increased inflow of low-cost imports from Eastern Europe will tend adversely to affect those EU regions which specialise in the production of similar goods, which in the main will be the already weaker and less developed regions, especially those where steel and textile production is important, or those which produce agricultural products at relatively low levels of efficiency. Most of these vulnerable areas tend to be in the south of the Community, in Greece, the Mezzogiorno, Spain and Portugal. Some negative results of competition with Eastern Europe are already visible. Sectors such as steel production (in Northern Italy and the Basque Country) are losing markets, while labour-intensive sectors such as textiles, clothing and processed food show tendencies to relocate from Greek regions to Bulgaria and Albania.

In the Mediterranean states which are not community members (MNCs), the problem takes a different dimension. The strong growth of population in relation to economic performance means that MNCs face a difficult problem of ensuring a sufficient rate of job creation to match the prospective increase in those looking for work, let alone providing employment for the many millions who are at present unemployed or working in the informal sector, particularly women. Population has grown continuously and consistently at around 2.5 per cent a year during the past 25 years. By 2025, it is projected to reach 345 millions, the same as the present population of the EU.

In recent years, trade between MNCs and the Community has changed in favour of the latter. The trade balance of MNCs with the EU deteriorated between 1989 and 1993. Of the 12 MNC countries, only Algeria and Libya had positive trade balances, and these were due to oil exports. But the major problem lies in the structure of the trade itself. The interregional trade in the Mediterranean, as

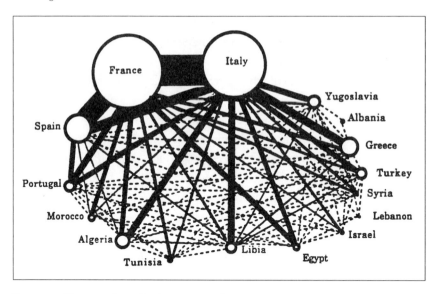

Diagram 1. The unequal inter-Mediterranean trade (import-export) in 1990

shown in diagram 1, takes place primarily among the rich countries of the northern shore (France, Italy), and only to a lesser extent between the northern shore and the south and south-eastern shores. 'Internal' trade relations among MNCs are very weak. These are, indeed, post-colonial or neo-colonial relations: natural resources (primarily oil and natural gas), vegetables, fruits and low technology industrial products *versus* manufactured goods, high technology and processed food and drinks. The main problem is that MNCs specialise in the same products and compete among themselves for EU markets, while trade with the EU is essential to their economies. In contrast, EU countries can interrupt their relation with partners along the Mediterranean African coast and in the Middle East without much loss. This is why 'the danger of massive immigration and a retreat into protectionism' is noted as the major implication of the further development of economic and political relations between the EU and the MNCs (European Parliament, COM-72, 1995). Consequently, the importance of supporting 'economic development, progress towards democracy, improving infrastructure and protecting the environment' is argued, while no references are made to human rights and military aggressiveness. This is the rationale for a number of current experimental programmes (such as MEDUNIV, MEDURBS and MEDINVEST). On the other hand, direct Community aid from the budget to MNCs (until 1995) accounted only for 0.1 per cent of

GNP and it has not until now had any significant macroeconomic effect.

The discussion so far can be summarised using the four tables below. These present some figures for the EU, MNCs and Eastern Europe (without Russia). We can conclude that the major problems/opportunities for the EU are: (a) the population 'threat' from the south, in combination with the high proportion of the existing immigrant population in the Community which originates from this area; (b) the wealth gap separating the EU and the two other areas, particularly the Mediterranean, in which a present wealth gap of 1:10 could become 1:20 by 2025; and (c) the preference of the west to invest in Central-Eastern Europe which offers two major resources: a cheap, well-trained workforce boasting near-German productivity levels, and an industrial/agricultural tradition close to mainstream

Figures for the EU, MNCs and Eastern Europe (without Russia)

Table 1 Population (millions)	1992	2010
EU	347	376
Mediterranean	209	304
Centr.,Eastern Europe	110	116

Table 2 Per capita GDP	1992	
EU	19,242 $	
Mediterranean	1,589 $	
Centr.,Eastern Europe	1,927 $	

Table 3 Direct foreign investment	1992	
Mediterranean	751 mil. ECU	
Centr.,Eastern Europe	1.612 mil. ECU	

Table 4 Immigrants in EU	1992	
From Mediterranean	4.6 million	
From Eastern Europe	0.7 million	

Source: Europe 2000+ (1994) FAST Dossier (1994)

European values. Culture, religion and politics are once again thoroughly interrelated, and this may leave the Mediterranean, including some Mediterranean regions of EU member states, with substantially less resources and opportunities.

Constructed meanings and processes of inclusion/exclusion

New globalised relations demand that the EU strengthen its position vis-a-vis the other two mega-regions of the world - the USA and Japan/Southeast Asia. These new relations are often used to legitimate two important geographical and social tendencies in prospect for the next ten to fifteen years: (a) a growing polarisation within the EU; a fact already acknowledged by most Community experts; and (b) the construction of new relations of inclusion/exclusion - leading often to crypto-colonialism - in relation to the 'outsiders' in the East and across the Mediterranean.

T he much advocated and discussed process of globalisation, a symbol of the new post-modern times, is not at all global in terms of bringing people together and distributing globally the fruits of development and prosperity. Many new aspects of globalisation are restricted to north-western, white, mostly male and Catholic/Protestant minorities, who travel and communicate at an accelerating rate.[1] Capital and information flow easily from certain places to other places - which happen to be those called developed capitalist regions. The existence of developed centres brings with it the abandonment and exclusion of others. Relations between global cities, global regions, global economic and military networks, as well as relations between the 'triad' (USA, EU, Japan/Southeast Asia) and the rest of the world, increasingly take the form of neo-colonial relations. What takes place is a selective global de-linking and the old 'concrete walls' or 'iron curtains' are replaced on the one hand by new electronic lines of demarcation and on the other by 'traditional' material ones based on the power of trade.

In this process 'constructed meanings', and the role of global media in particular, are instrumental in the distribution of acceptable practices, and the legitimation of cultural identities. The unequal relations among EU, Eastern European and Mediterranean countries are founded, among other things, on constructed meanings (perhaps dating back to the eleventh century), in which the EU, and in particular its north-central part, stands as the powerful and unquestionable centre.

---

1. D. Massey, *Space, Place and Gender*, Polity Press, Oxford 1994.

A key category here is the debatable notion of 'European identity'. What today motivates dominant ideas about European identity is the desire to exclude the Other - those ideas, meanings and practices which do not fit with a Eurocentric vision, those intruders who are not from 'European stock'.[2] Eurocentrism, according to Edward Said, imposes 'imaginative geographies' which dominate the representation of space, as well as social practices; in these the centre is powerful, articulate, surveillant, the subject who is making history; while the periphery is defeated, silenced, subordinate, the subjected, without a history of its own. A hidden process seems to be at work which Cornelius Castoriadis pin-points as:

> the apparent incapacity to constitute oneself as oneself without excluding the other - *and* the apparent inability to exclude the other without devaluing and ultimately, hating him.[3]

Of course the ideology of European cultural superiority is not new and can be traced back to Ancient Greece and Rome. What *is* new, however, is the search for deep historical roots able to prove that this superiority was achieved primarily as a result of 'internal reasons' which favoured Europe within the global system. This constructed meaning has a distinct dual political and cultural project: cultural homogenisation within Europe proper and a model of 'catching-up' for the outsiders. The classic expression of both of these notions is the measurement of performance of each country, region or social group against the 'developed' ones, using 'international development indices'. Despite criticism, this approach still dominates development thinking and policies. It is part of the wider project of constructed meanings, since all measure their success or failure against the white, male, Catholic/Protestant, north-central European/American capitalist ideal.

The official language of the EU is also significant: it is the language of cohesion, integration, unity, community and security. The new European order, and its relations with Eastern and Mediterranean states, is being constructed in terms of an idealised wholeness and plenitude in which geographies and societies appear

---

2. See E. Said, 'Orientalism Reconsidered', in F. Barker *et al* (eds), *Europe and its Others*, Univ. of Essex, Colchester 1985 and; S. Amin, *Eurocentrism*, Zed Books, London 1989.
3. C. Castoriadis, *Le Monde Morcele,* Seuil, Paris 1990, cited in K. Robins, A. Aksoy, 'Culture and marginality in the New Europe', in Hadjimichalis and Sadler (eds), *Europe at the Margins: New Mosaics of Inequality*, J.Wiley, Chichester 1995.

only as the bounded space of Eurocentrism. These meanings and modes of inclusion within and exclusion from Europe, have been powerfully shaped over the centuries by the historical and spatial experience of building nation states. The principle, or the aspiration, has been that of homogeneity, ethnic, religious, linguistic, cultural but not economic, political and spatial. Monolithic and inward looking, the nation state was a closed cultural entity.

Here is where Bosnia matters, as Robins and Aksoy remind us. Unlike other parts of Europe, Bosnia continued to evolve a culture which expressed the plural and tolerant side of the Ottoman tradition. It has struggled over the past years to defend the values of a multi-cultural, multi-meaning, long-evolved and mutually fruitful cohabitation. As in Cyprus twenty-two years ago, the genocide in Bosnia was directed against a unique European society which had not been homogenised - it was not 'like us'. Europeans, and the EU as a political entity, by accepting the destruction of Bosnia - some for cynical geopolitical interest, some due to ignorance - have damaged (some even say they have killed) both the project of European integration and the opening towards the East and the Mediterranean. Bosnia was a microcosm of what we find today in many Eastern states and the Moslem Mediterranean. Its destruction, after the Gulf War, has aggravated the problems of countries and people in the Balkans, the ex-Soviet Union and the Mediterranean. It has created in large segments of Arab and Christian Orthodox societies a crisis of confidence in Europe, far deeper than any known so far.[4] Then, too, anti-Arab and, to a lesser degree, anti-Orthodox (via images of 'butcher' Serbs) sentiment in Europe is on the rise, aggravating the problems of acceptance and integration facing migrant workers, and leading to racial intolerance and xenophobia.

New frontiers are thus being established at a time when everyone speaks of their destruction in globalised new times. Since German unification the idea of *Mitteleuropa* has been revived which, if one associates it with proposals for two-speed European integration, may construct a quite possible scenario of inclusion/exclusion. Outsiders from the EU, and some insiders as well, today face a process similar to that which involved the *limes* of the Roman Empire against the 'Barbarians' - those 'non-civilised persons who cannot speak Latin properly and defend themselves in front of the Senate'.[5] The new *limes*

4. See *The Guardian*, 6.12.95.

will encompass existing north-central EU member states and, to the East, will include regions of the former Austro-Hungarian and Prussian empires; from the Balkans, Slovenia and Croatia are included (note that Greece is excluded); Italy will be inside but maybe not to the south of Rome, the Iberian peninsula perhaps as far as Madrid or Seville, and the British Isles, perhaps without Ireland. The new *limes* could broadly follow those of the Great Schism of 1054 between Rome and Constantinople (see map opposite). The criteria of inclusion/exclusion would once again be cultural and religious and both Orthodoxy (Russians, Serbs, Roumanians, Bulgarians, Greeks) and Islam (Bosnians, Albanians, Turks, Arabs of Middle East and North Africa) would be excluded, would constitute the *Other,* that cannot belong to essential Europe. This symbolic/imaginary exclusion also involves more material forms, as north-central EU regions prepare to close their gates to millions of immigrants, to welcome selectively certain imports while excluding others, and to secure trade, financial and tourist flows to these Other places. In this respect, this exclusion of the new 'Barbarians', is not a cutting of Europe from its surroundings. It is intended rather to dominate them, to include them as inferiors.

This new *limes* works inside the Europe of the fifteen as well, making the above scenario even more possible. Today a new wall of poverty and marginalisation runs right through all the member states. The meta-fordist social contract of negotiable involvement in north-central Europe, and the family/small business/informal economy model in southern Europe, are both in crisis. In the early 1990s 58 million people were considered to be 'poor' (one third of the Europe of the 12), 3 million were homeless and 15 million formally unemployed. And not all people who work and live in Europe can have now the right to citizenship. Neo-racism builds new inner boundaries and excludes the '16th state': 12.5 million foreign *demizens* and *immigrants,* a map you can't draw. In addition, many women, particularly in the south, work in the informal sector, without normal payment and social security, without the acceptance by employers and the unions of their status as 'workers'. Because of this lack, they are nowhere near the image of the 'social partner', whose role in dialogue is heavily promoted

---

5. *Limes* is a Latin term in the singular, describing the geopolitical and cultural boundary of the Roman Empire. It was at the same time symbolic/imaginary and material, taking more tangible forms when needed. See S. Ruffin, *L' empire et les nouveax barbares,* Lattes, Paris 1991.

Frontiers of the Great Schism of 1054
Frontiers of the Austro-Hungarian Empire
Frontiers of the nation-states since World War II

Map 1: Historical frontiers on which the new limes are based

by the EU.[6] Thus, an exclusion is established from the outset: millions of these women cannot have a voice in the coming negotiations.

Racial and gender divisions also restrict the freedom of mobility - a much celebrated fruit of the Single Market. There is seldom, in European pronouncements, any reference to everyday life, to those differentiated 'lived spaces' of Europeans, to the unequal terms of integration of places, races and genders. Social limits to mobility are insufficiently recognised, and the false assumption prevails that constructing more technical infrastructures will solve the problem. But such policies work in support of the few white, north-central men, who congest Euro-terminals, busily talking in their mobile telephones. Their hyper-mobility relies on the stasis of all the others who have contributed (directly or indirectly) for these expensive infrastructures and who are forced to stay behind these new inner boundaries of exclusion.

Concluding comment: a two-front 'Mexicanisation'?

During the Davos International Economic Summit in February 1996, Jeffrey Jacks from Harvard University, made a comparison between Mexico and Eastern Europe (*Guardian*, 8.2.96). He argued that, just as the USA and Canada have found in neighbouring Mexico a source of cheap labour, cheap energy and agricultural inputs (as did Japan in Southeast Asia), today a similar golden opportunity is open to Europe in ex-socialist countries of the East. However, he urged Europeans to 'do it properly' and avoid the USA's mistakes, mistakes which turned Mexico in six months from '*l'enfant gâté*' of the West to an almost bankrupt country.

By extending Jacks's scenario to the Mediterranean, we may in fact predict a two-front 'Mexicanisation': the creation of a buffer zone both to the east and to the south of the EU, echoing the old *limes*, which would be a source of controlled immigration, cheap energy and agricultural inputs, and demand for European products, accommodation for mass tourism and the location of industries (the equivalent of '*maquilladoras*'?). This potential reorganisation of European and Mediterranean space would strengthen north-central European regions but would further marginalise southern ones (see map 2 overleaf).

---

6. D. Vaiou, 'Women of the South after, like before, Maastricht ?', in Hadjimichalis and Sadler (eds), *op.cit.*

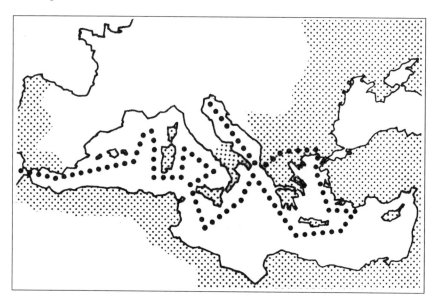

Map 2: The EU border which immigrants from the Southern Mediterranean have to cross (dotted line) and the 'buffer zone' of two-front Mexicanisation based on current socio-economic performance and historical/cultural frontiers of the past (tinted area).

Political forces opposing this scenario seem to be weak, and dispersed among the regions and social groups most affected. Hopes for organisation do exist, but they require a progressive and radical 'openness', and acceptance of the Other as equal, instead of a defensive and nationalistic closure. At the first meeting since the era of Eurocommunism of left and radical European political forces in Paris in May 1996, there was a serious attempt to open the discussion on these issues. But, although combatting racism and discrimination against foreign immigrants seems to be already part of the common ground for alternative left wing policies, issues such as gender, spatial differences and cultural marginalisation - not to speak of religion - are still way off the agenda of the majority of parties which participated in the Paris meeting.

Similar problems exist among left forces in the European Parliament. There is much discussion of traditional regional and welfare policies 'helping' peripheral regions and social groups, and little awareness of the wider processes of marginalisation which are shaping the New Europe. This is where a new kind of left argument is needed. On the one hand we have to fight and defend against neoliberalism our achievements - the welfare state, employment, living standards. (In many parts of Europe, everyday living conditions seem to have returned to the nineteenth century, making a focus only on postmodern consumptionist issues rather ironic.) On the other hand, we have to open up these new issues - of more refined marginalisation and exclusion, of culture and religion - and discuss seriously how they could be inserted into current EU policies, and how we might cope with them. It is urgent, as a first step, to convince ourselves, and to convince our friends and comrades in north-central Europe, that these issues are real and that we need common efforts to draw up alternative policies.

Of special value here is the spatial feminist and postcolonial critique of Gloria Anzaldúa, whose major work on borderlands between Mexico and the USA sets the scene.[7] Anzaldúa proposes a move 'beyond an homogenising globalisation, to the persistent recognition of heterogeneity', to organise ourselves for radical resistance. This resistence can take many forms in which the formulation of new categories and new meanings plays a key role. She offers her own first step:

> We need theories that will rewrite history using race, class, gender and ethnicity as categories of analysis, theories that cross borders, that blur boundaries.... Because not only we are not allowed to enter in the West, we are not allowed to enter discourse, because we are often disqualified or excluded from dominant meanings, because what passes for theory these days is forbidden territory for us

There are many more forbidden territories, both actual and imaginary, and the process of European 'integration' seems to multiply them. Our agenda must include both their conquest and the attempt to eliminate their reproduction.

---

7. G. Anzaldúa, *Making Face, Making Soul, Haciendo Caras*, Univ. of California Press, San Francisco 1990.

Ilse's German passport. It came back from being renewed stamped on the outside with a large red 'J' (for Jude), and the first name 'Sara' had been added. The Nazis named all Jewish women Sara and all men Israel.

German reconcilings

A trip to Berlin becomes a passage between a mother and a daughter, racisms old and new, East and West, past and present.

Miriam Glucksmann

The door half-opened to reveal a naked man. He eyed me suspiciously, keeping the door on the chain, as I repeated my request in halting German.

'My mother used to live in this house for many years before the War. I'm visiting Berlin from England for the first time and would very much like to look around. Would it be possible for me to come and have a quick look inside your apartment?'

Success at last on the fourth floor! I had managed to gain access to the house by ringing first one, then two, and finally all the door bells outside until the front entrance door opened. Walking along L-Strasse, close to the centre of West Berlin, my quest seemed increasingly doomed. Either the house would no longer exist or it would have turned into a shopfront like most of the others. So once I'd got inside the front entrance hall I had to carry on. My mother, Ilse, had lived here with her agoraphobic mother and two older brothers, and later her stepfather, from the age of seven in 1916 until the early 1930s when her mother died. Not long afterwards she left Germany in search of work, thrown out of university in 1933 for being a Communist before she could complete her medical studies. She left Berlin for the last time on 31 December 1935 - for Denmark, followed by Belgium, Italy, Switzerland, and finally England where she arrived in November 1938 - seen off at the railway station by her boyfriend Werner, and Bruno, her second brother. She never saw Bruno again. He and his wife and daughter did not survive the Holocaust. But contact was re-established with Werner after the War. A non-Jew, member of the German Communist

Party, and active in the resistance, he later became a Volksdoktor in the GDR, living in East Berlin until after the fall of the Wall.

Conferences and unspoken differences

Retracing family history was not the reason for my being in Berlin. I had come for a conference on 'Women's employment since 1945 in comparative perspective', organised by German contemporary social historians. The main focus was comparison of married women's paid work in the former East and West Germanies, against the context of other western European and eastern bloc countries. But, as many say of the reunification process itself, the Federal Republic dominated. Most participants came from the West, even if they now lived in, studied or held academic positions in the East. The majority of papers also concerned the experience of the FRG. After three intensive days I had learned much about women in post-war Germany, and a lot more German than the household vocabulary with which I'd come - inadequately - equipped, having presumptuously expected the conference to be in English.

But my overwhelming feeling at the end of the conference was puzzlement - as to why many of the German women academics were reluctant to discuss migrant workers; and why, while the concept of a gendered division of labour was unproblematic, the question of ethnic divisions in the labour force should be so strongly resisted or treated as irrelevant. Reinforcing this perplexity, on a different plane, was the fact that while all the other 'foreign' participants had asked about my background (prompted no doubt by the combination of a German-sounding name and an inability to speak German), none of the Germans asked. Did they just not notice or were they not curious? Were they embarrassed or wanting to avoid a possibility of being guilt-tripped about the past? Or, in even thinking this, was I projecting my own lifelong embarrassment onto them? Whatever the reason, I was perplexed by the almost uniformly dismissive response to issues of racism and ethnicity, and this was to filter the perception of my remaining days looking around Berlin.

Addressing my mother's past

When I had first arrived at 'my mother's house' I had knocked on the solid door of the first floor flat on the right - which I knew was my mother's flat - and a young man came out. He had a moustache and pony tail, was wearing shorts, and smoking, and looked rather hostile. Ironic that I should now be actively volunteering to this unknown man the family history about which I normally remain silent. He had stared blankly as I blurted out my request, and did not respond to further persistence. 'Can't you just look at the entrance area of the house and take photos of the stairs?' I'd come at a bad time. He was too busy watching football on TV. England was playing - against Scotland, in the first round of the Euro 96 championship. But he had also made clear that there would be no convenient time.

So now, naked man or not, I wanted to take whatever chance there was of gaining entry to the top floor flat. Momentarily, while the man went to get dressed, I thought that perhaps this was not such a brilliant idea after all, attempting to barge into a strange man's home, especially as I hadn't even told anyone where I was going. But I was driven. I'd got this far and was absolutely determined to get inside. I'd heard so much about my mother's childhood in this house: the old tiled stove, the only source of heating, on which her older brother Arthur had written maths formulae; the tiny damp 'Mädchenzimmer' (maid's room) where my mother slept, which was so cold that icicles 'grew' on the walls in winter; the balcony where she read in the summer; the lodger whose rent helped support a widow with three children. There had been a prison close by, and my mother remembered the prisoners coming into the street when they were freed by amnesty during the abortive revolution in 1918. Later, she heard crowds shouting in the street that 'Die Hexe ist tot' ('the witch is dead') after Rosa Luxemburg had been assassinated. Across the road was the dairy where her mother sent her to buy milk, afraid to leave the house herself, and twenty minutes walk away was her school, ever illustrious in memory, the Fürstin Bismarck Schule. Her beloved grandmother lived in nearby P- Strasse with her unmarried daughter Tante Terese.

After repeating my story in ever greater detail in English and German, explaining exactly who I was and showing my card, the man finally said he would ask his wife if I could come in. Great relief on both counts! And, as luck would have it, I fell on my feet with Rolf and Gabriele, a couple in their mid-thirties. Not only were they librarians with a strong interest in local history, but their flat retained many of its original features, including not one but two stoves, both elaborately decorated with beautiful coloured tiles and figurines, although no longer used for heating. They looked like altars in a baroque church. The balcony was still there, but the 'Mädchenzimmer' was now incorporated into the kitchen.

Ceiling-high double doors, with art nouveau mouldings, linked the two main rooms. And all the fittings, which must have dated from the late nineteenth century, retained their original style. The 'out of the past' effect was reinforced by the present occupants' collection of '*Gründerzeit*' furniture, dating from the first period of German unification around 1870. It was all much plusher, more comfortable and larger than suggested by my mother's account of her poverty-stricken childhood.

Once Rolf and Gabriele believed my story they became extremely helpful, offering a mine of information, treating my quest as quite an adventure. They showed books of old postcards of Charlottenburg from the 1910s, and of architecture and interior design of the turn of the century. They described the original black and white stone kitchen floor tiles which they had replaced, and took me down the back stairs to the courtyard. In the early days this must have been the entrance for tradesmen and servants, but it was now no longer in use and in a neglected state, looking much more like the drab bare wooden steps and peeling brown plastered walls of my imagination. They were keen to contact the owner of the house on my behalf for a copy of the records detailing my grandmother's rental contract. Close by there had indeed been a prison, which remained a remand centre for girls until 1985. It was a tall white and green building with an ornate roof and cupolas, easily mistaken for a normal house if you ignored the imperial eagle-embossed sign near the top. A friend of theirs is curator of a Jewish local history museum in the Mitte district of former East Berlin and they suggested arranging to meet him. Along with other things English (including a collection of Inspector Morse and Steptoe and Son videos), tea was with Marks and Spencer biscuits brought back from a recent trip to London, and was followed by a longer account of my parents' lives and the circumstances in which they had left Germany. Rolf and Gabriele then insisted on accompanying me to my mother's school.

As we walked, more fragments of my mother's story surfaced in my mind. How she was always hungry as a child, and eligible for free '*Quäker Speisung*' at school after the First World War, a delicious bowl of something warm, sweet and filling, which she recognised decades later in England as rice pudding. The kindness of her grandmother whom she visited nearly every day. My mother does not know what happened to Tante Terese but fears the worst. There is nothing left to

Ilse's first day at school, Berlin, April 1915.

Ilse, on the right, aged 9, her grandmother Bertha Weinstock, and the torn-out Tante Terese, Berlin 1918

remember her by: Terese herself had torn her face out of the only photo my mother had of her and her grandmother. Tante Terese would have been about seventy when they bade farewell at the end of 1935. Her brother Bruno had pressed a 5 mark coin into my mother's hand at the station, and she had pressed it back into Werner's as you were not allowed to take money out of the country. The hands of the clock were at midnight as the train drew out of the station and into 1936.

On the way to the school Rolf and Gabriele pointed out local landmarks and many plaques commemorating Jewish cultural centres and homes, and spoke of their own parents' experience of the Hitler period. No embarrassment here at all. Unlike the conference participants, Rolf and Gabriele seemed entirely open and at ease talking to me about German history and I (unusually) did not feel I was making myself vulnerable by revealing my family past. The puzzle deepened. Was this the new generation of younger Germans? (I know one cannot generalise.) Or did anti-anti-semitism have no implication for thinking about the situation of 'foreign' workers and residents in post-war Germany? A pity, I thought in retrospect, that I didn't talk to them about the Turks in present-day Berlin. But they sent me a strongly anti-Hitler e-mail back home.

In fact I could almost have guided Rolf and Gabriele to the school. At 88 my mother can still reel off the exact route from L- Strasse to the school in H- Strasse, with all the left and right turns and street crossings. In her estimation, the prestigious girls' grammar school that I had attended in the 1960s was not a patch on the Fürstin Bismarck Schule of the 1910s and 1920s, either in facilities or breadth of education. Mine had no gym, and only old fashioned science labs. No organic chemistry was taught nor modern literature. From an early age I had known how my mother loved jumping over the horse and swinging on the rings whilst I was so bad at gym. She had read Colette's *Chérie* at school in French literature, while the most modern author we read was Gide. She thought all I ever seemed to learn about in history (three times over) was the Tudors and Stuarts, while she had acquired a systematic grasp of the chronology of European and world history from the Greeks onward.

The physical appearance did not live up to the image implanted in my mind. All was closed and silent and there were no children about, on a Saturday afternoon. I had always 'seen' the school as a modern building full of light and air but in fact it was gloomy, dark, heavy, giving a strong sense of foreboding. It was a six-storey building of rectangular concrete blocks, shaped into mock rock to look like a pyramid or amphitheatre. Originally white, it was now in urgent need of cleaning. Inscriptions in Greek and gargoyle-like statues, mostly headless, were visible near the top if you craned your head backwards. Without the sign to indicate that it had been built in 1857 the building could easily be mistaken as a typical example of fascist or stalinist architecture. But it is still a school, now renamed the Sophie Charlotte Oberschule. My mother refused to believe it was the same school until shown the photo of the main entrance which she recognised. 'You wouldn't believe my school still looks so good', she says, 'not a nasty building like yours'. Too many impressions, and no time to process them. I was due to meet a Scandinavian colleague from the conference at one of the big museums on Unter den Linden, quite a distance away, and had no idea where I was or how to get there. I dissuaded Rolf and Gabriele from taking me there themselves and after exchanging e-mail addresses, and with profuse thanks on my part, we said goodbye, and I took the 100 bus to Unter den Linden.

I later discovered that a trip on the 100 bus is highly recommended for viewing the sights of Berlin. So it was a lucky chance again that I sat at the front on the top. It passed the Presidential Palace, the Tiergarten park (lots of Turkish families picnicking here, including many women, I noted, defiantly, who must be working in one way or another), Platz der Republik (a very large hole in the ground), the Reichstag, and the Brandenburg Gate, before turning into the famous Unter den Linden which had none of the evocative atmosphere that might have been expected, nor any lime trees either. I clutched my map anxiously trying to work out where we were until the elderly man sitting next to me explained the route. He took this bus regularly, he said, but was always amazed that where buildings had been standing one week there was only an enormous hole in the ground the following week. Alighting at the State Opera House I hardly noticed the large grouping of grandiose Prussian cultural buildings, theatres, museums, the Humboldt University, and former East German seats of government. I was intent on finding a phone box. Full of excitement I rang my mother to tell her I'd just been in 'her' house.

'But the flat where I lived was on the first floor on the right. Did you go in there?' That was where England had been playing football.

'No', I had to confess. 'I couldn't get in there but I did go in one on the fourth floor and, guess what, they still had the original stoves.'

'But that was the wrong flat. I lived on the first floor.'

My mother's and my relationship in a nutshell.

Tracing racisms

My mother was a highly qualified scientist, engaged in research on cancer of the lung and prostate, developing techniques of tissue and organ culture. She

Ilse, safe in England, 1940, reading The New Yorker

would have liked to have been a doctor but by the time the British authorities relaxed the bar on those with foreign medical degrees it was too late. Unlike the mothers of my friends she worked full-time throughout my childhood.

At a reunion of my school class, it was staggering to learn that, out of sixty, I and perhaps four or five others were the only ones in full-time employment. This was the school that had looked down on anyone who did not go to Oxbridge, and had drummed into its pupils strict standards of academic excellence and the importance of an independent career. My now middle-aged classmates all came out with the same half-hearted line, that their education had not been wasted because they were 'handing it on to their children'. Big deal, I thought, and what about *their* daughters? Most depressing was the girl who wanted to be a brain surgeon now married to a brain surgeon. Going over my mother's photos of her school friends, it appeared that a higher proportion (of those who survived) pursued careers themselves. A photo of seven fifteen year olds includes two future psychoanalysts, one doctor, one who was killed fighting in the Spanish Civil War, an artist and my mother. A highly unrepresentative bunch of female German school graduates of the class of 1926!

Two future psychoanalysts, two future doctors, an artist, and a casuality-to-be of the Spanish Civil War. Ilse (on the far left) with a group of fifteen year old schoolfriends, Berlin, 1924.

My long-standing interest in women's work is no doubt 'not unconnected' to all this background, but I wouldn't put it more strongly than that.

Here I was, at a conference in Berlin, attempting to reconcile tales of my mother's past with my present impressions, but the attempt was becoming confused with - or by - coming to terms with the conference itself. Why the glaring absence of discussions on migrants, ethnicity and racism from the workshops? It is almost inconceivable that a conference in Britain in 1996 on 'Women's employment since 1945 in comparative perspective' would not include papers on different ethnic groups, or that questions concerning the dynamics connecting 'racial' and gender processes would not be central. And if previous impressions were correct, this was not just a chance omission. At European-wide socialist feminist conferences in the 1980s where racism had been a major issue, German participants were noted for being impervious to the debate. I clearly remember one respected German feminist theorist authoritatively asserting that racism was an issue neither in the German women's movement nor in Germany.

Surely women's different pattern of economic participation in the GDR might have raised questions about the significance of foreign workers in the West? In the GDR it had been normal for married women and mothers to remain permanently in the workforce and to work full-time. But in the FRG the 'breadwinner/housewife ideology' remained strong until the late 1960s and 1970s. Had this any connection with the '*Gastarbeiter*' system which brought so many foreign workers into the West on short-term contracts?

German nationality laws (or are they even now ethnicity laws?) have prevented many 'foreign' residents and their German-born children and grandchildren from claiming German citizenship, and perpetuate the construction of millions of the resident population (who under British laws would have become or been born British citizens) as 'foreign'. Hence news reports in the media documented attacks on 'Turks' rather than on 'Germans' or 'Germans of Turkish descent'. The bodies of Turkish women killed in an arson attack in 1993 were described as being sent 'home' for burial even though most were 'third generation' Turkish-Germans.

The exclusion of Turkish and other descended residents from German citizenship by laws governing nationality was reflected in their parallel exclusion, by this assembly of social scientists, from being a part of the analysis of German society. Several participants turned the discussion back on me; they argued that, while the history of early post-war employment in the UK was undoubtedly tied up with decolonisation of the Empire which also brought colonial migrants to Britain, the situation in Germany had been quite different. Not only had it not been a colonial country, but the *Gastarbeiter* system developed only slowly towards the end of the 1950s, and it was much later, in the late 1960s and 1970s, that the 'wives of immigrants' were drawn into the labour market. Well, yes, of course, I thought, different countries have different histories of racism and colonialism, and the way the past affects the present is bound to vary. But that does not mean it is irrelevant. I came away with the impression that, for many of these German academics, racism was associated with the Nazi past. The study of migration was separate, a legitimate subject, but definitely a different discipline, with few implications for researchers on women's employment.

It would be quite misleading to suggest that a narrow definition of racism - belonging to the pre-war period and characterised primarily by anti-semitism - and the sharp distinction drawn between the Nazi and post-war eras, have prevented all Germans from recognising the significance of ethnic relations of domination and division in their recent history. Quite apart from left politicians, anti-racist activists, and those involved in defending asylum seekers today, Fassbinder's film *Fear Eats the Soul* dealt directly with the issue, as did Wallraff's account of his own treatment at the hands of co-citizens when he pretended to be a Turk.[1] It forms the sub-theme of many of Heinrich Böll's novels. And, I discovered after my return, groups in Hamburg and at Berlin's Technical University are researching contemporary racism. Nevertheless, the hasty impression I had gained is echoed by one of these very researchers:

Racism is identified with genocide. This is the past. It is a horrid, an unfathomable, non-repeatable mistake. The concept of racism has been ignored within mainstream academic discourse and has had no place within university curricula, nor has it been on the agenda for social scientific research.[2]

But this was June 1996, do not forget. At home Round One in the 'ban-on-British-beef war' was just coming to a head, and Euro 96 was in full swing. The British

1. Günter Wallraff, *The Lowest of the Low*, Methuen, London 1988.
2. Czarina Wilpert, 'Ideological and institutional foundations of racism in the Federal Republic of Germany', in John Wrench and John Solomos (eds), *Racism and Migration in Western Europe*, Berg, Oxford 1993.

tabloids turned both into excuses for the most extreme stereotyping and racist abuse of Germans. The Labour-supporting *Daily Mirror* outstripped others in its virulent attacks on the supposed national characteristics of one country after another. The most venomous were reserved for Germany in the run-up to the semi-final, when the headline read 'Achtung! Surrender. For you Fritz, ze Euro 96 championship is over', while inside readers were regaled by 'Mirror declares football war on Germany', by The Editor. Not much better were 'Give 'em Heil!', 'For Klin the war is over', 'Herr we go. Bring on the Kraut', and 'Hun Beatable'. England lost, of course. But that was not the point.

Instead of concentrating on why BSE was an essentially British disease, Tory politicians and the tabloids descended into nationalistic, anti-European, and, above all, anti-German hysteria over the beef ban. One front page headline, complete with photo of Churchill giving the V sign, read 'The cattle of Britain. Never in the field of human conflict has so much beef been banned from so many by so few'. Another, rehearsing wartime allusions to plucky little Britain, asked 'Who do you think you are kidding, Chancellor Kohl?'; a third showed an unflattering photo of Chancellor Kohl with the caption 'Kohl eating our beef with a forked tongue'.

Returning to my hotel room late on that Saturday evening, a news magazine programme on German television devoted a special slot to anti-German sentiment in the British media. 'Why do the English need to do this?', the presenters asked, looking at the TV advert for lager shown at that time in Britain (lager going with football of course) which played on Dambusters nostalgia, showing slim muscular Englishmen unfurling the Union Flag and diving athletically into the water after cans of lager, while red-faced pot-bellied elderly Germans arrived too late at the water to get any beer, out of breath, running clumsily down the stairs and bumping into each other. 'All good fun...not meant to be true', or words to that effect, said the advert maker when interviewed by the German reporter: 'no need to take it so seriously'. The reporter's comment to the German audience was 'true, Britannia may once have ruled the waves, but now it's only a hotel swimming pool'. The sentiment was echoed by Helmut Schmidt the following month in a BBC 2 programme made by the London reporter of *Die Zeit*.[3] According to the former Chancellor, the vitriolic xenophobia said far more about the British than the Germans, particularly the formers' inability to adapt to the loss of an imperial and global role.

3. Jürgen Kronig of *Die Zeit*, *Don't Mention the War*, BBC 2, 8 July 1996.

Photos of stone

The following day was my last full one, and I planned a bit of leisurely exploration in former East Berlin. Friends had recommended the marvellous museums; but they will still be there in a few years, I thought, whereas East Berlin might change completely. My first impression, on looking round side streets and courtyards off Oranienburger Strasse, was of elegant decay, buildings of distinctive brown brick, many of which were crumbling and in disrepair, old-fashioned street and shop signs. It was easy to imagine how it would have looked in the 1950s or even the 1930s. One alleyway led to a leafy courtyard which would have been an outdoor cafe if the old wooden trestle tables and fold-up chairs were anything to go by. Strains of live jazz wafted out of the open windows. Was this a music school or cultural centre? And a basement art shop specialised in postcard replicas of the scene: photos of old bicycles leant against a crumbling brick wall, of graffiti in the stairwell of a local apartment house, of dilapidated houses in cobbled streets, all mixed up with old black and white postcards of Berlin trams in the 1920s, railway stations and the Reichstag in the 1930s, of a young woman sunbathing in the early 1950s, her hammock slung between the ruins of two buildings in a bomb site. No doubting that the postcard industry was trading on nostalgia, even to the extent of turning the present into the past. But the new cards definitely captured something of the atmosphere of the area - the sense, to someone coming from the West at least, of entering an island from the past, even if the other side of the main road was bustling with a flea market.

This street had housed the New Synagogue, one of the largest in Berlin during the early twentieth century, burned on Kristallnacht, bombed in 1943, and finally demolished in 1958. It was now being rebuilt, its large blue and gold cupolas complementing the famous East Berlin TV tower on the skyline. It had reopened only a month previously as the Centrum Judaicum, a museum of Jewish life in Berlin and was guarded by armed police and extremely strict security. In these days such buildings are necessarily protected by a German uniformed presence, it seems.

After some dithering I went in. I did not want to get dragged back into 'all that past', and definitely not into any with a religious connotation. So I made for the old photographs, unprepared for the emotional impact of a collection of old slides in a push-button display. Here were groups of women and girls pictured working in kitchens, peeling potatoes, washing up, stacking saucepans, eating in communal dining rooms, sewing. Many of the photos seemed to have been taken in children's homes, established, presumably, for children who had lost parents in the First World War or the short-lived revolution. The children were snapped unposed, at school, playing with toys, dressed up for a party, walking in the street. Most family groups had been taken at home, but some were formal studio portraits. All were black and white, dating from around 1915 until 1930.

The people looked so familiar and suddenly I realised why. They could have been straight out of the family photos I had known since I was a small child. The people here looked just like uncles, mothers, cousins, grandparents in my parents' old photos. These relatives, whose names and history I know, although I never knew them, could have been any of the people in the slide show. Suddenly I saw them anew in my mind's eye, not simply as the old family photos of 'my' family but in their historical context: no longer my mother's brothers or my father's parents or cousins (my father was also an exile from Nazi Germany), but people just like the nameless, also long-lost, people of these photographs, who had lived, and died, in the same awful circumstance.

A reconstruction of the neighbourhood showed that 26, Grosser Hamburger Strasse, just around the corner, had been a rounding-up point for the deportation of Berlin Jews. I had to see if it was still there. Soon after the war, my mother had written to the Berlin city authorities for information about Bruno. A swift reply, brief but to the point, gave the precise date, in March 1942, when Bruno Lasnitzki had been sent on 'Ost Transport'. His wife and fourteen year old daughter followed one week later. At the same time as explaining over and over again why it had been impossible for her to help get Bruno out of Germany (this unnecessary guilt seems more pronounced in Holocaust survivors as they get older), my mother still frequently remarks on her surprise at the 'systematic records'. She cannot get over it. 'Can you imagine that the Nazis kept such records? They had the exact date for Bruno, and for Etti and Susi. They must have written down the details of every single person.'

The corner of Oranienburger Strasse with Grosser Hamburger Strasse was another large hole in the ground. More demolition and more building site. The rest of the street looked as if it might well follow. There was a number 25 but definitely no number 26. Then I noticed the marble memorial stone set back from the street in a small green space with trees and benches. It stood about four foot high, bearing the inscription

This spot marks the site of the first old people's home of the Jewish Community. In 1942 the Gestapo turned it into a collection camp for Jewish citizens. 55,000 Berlin Jews, from babes in arms to the elderly, were dragged from here to the concentration camps of Auschwitz and Theresienstadt and brutally murdered.

And underneath in larger lettering

Never forget.
Defend against war.
Guard over peace.

Another lump in my throat. Bruno and family had quite probably been brought here and it was probably in Auschwitz that they had died. My father's parents 'perished' (the euphemism I grew up with) in Theresienstadt.

Now I took a photograph, manoeuvring to make sure that the whole of the stone fitted in the frame. As I stepped back, it was clear that a woman who had been walking from the other end of the street had waited for me to finish. She was youngish, with straight shoulder-length black hair, in sandals, and wearing a long red dress and sunglasses, not at all Jewish-looking. She placed a bunch of long-stemmed pink carnations on the top of the stone and carried on walking.

I waited until I saw my mother in person to tell her about my visit to the ex-New Synagogue, worried that all this would upset her. But her reaction appeared positively matter-of-

Memorial stone to Berlin's holocaust victims

fact: 'I really don't know why you bothered to go there. You know I was an atheist. I never went to a synagogue in my life. And, anyway I don't know that part of Berlin at all. I never went there.' But, the photo of the memorial stone is the only one to which she keeps returning.

The present never meets the past

Trams still run in East Berlin, and I caught one going north east. Prenzlauerberg already felt far away. In the 1920s it had been 'red'. Now the facades of its long rows of high Prussian houses were crumbling, confirming the earlier air of fashionable decay. A few had been restored, newly plastered and painted, providing a graphic image of 'before' and 'after', and a preview of future elegance, once property developers and former owners from the West have reclaimed the area. In the cobbled side streets were few shops, few trees and little traffic. But children were playing, unaccompanied by adults, and you could hear birds singing. It all seemed very quiet and peaceful. After the pushing and pulling of emotions I welcomed the tranquility. Old ladies were walking their dogs, and people leaned over their balconies taking in the view. A small boy was chalking a picture on the outside of a house.

Green and leafy Kollwitz Platz, well equipped with ping-pong tables, swings and sandpit, as well as its statue of Käthe Kollwitz, at first seemed like a traditional Sunday meeting place for people of all ages, unaffected by the changes. But, run by 'Westies', cafes and restaurants in surrounding streets produced a discordant sensation: cafe sitters watching the local people walking by, the local people watching the cafe sitters watching them, a discomforting meeting of East and West. Returning to the main road, I walked behind a young woman with peroxide beehive hair, wearing tight jeans and a pink orlon jumper, reminiscent of the archetypical Eastern bloc worker. She met a group of similarly dressed friends at the next junction and they continued on to Alexanderplatz. For no reason, suddenly I heard my mother telling of how she had gone to dump her volumes of Thomas Mann and 'Das Kapital' in a phone box; it was too dangerous to keep them or to give them away. En route, she was stopped by an SS officer. But he seemed interested only in chatting her up.

Just by the bus stop a doctors' surgery caught my eye: all seven of the doctors listed were women, specialists in different fields. Impossible to tell whether medicine had been a feminised low-status profession in the GDR, or whether the sign suggested rather the absence of rigid gender segregation. In any case, I wondered how these women were doing now. How had they been affected by the privatisation of primary health care? Such issues had been of marginal concern at the conference.

Back at the Museum Insel, I made for another photographic exhibition, showing in the German Historical Museum, this time because of its theme 'Views of Germany. Portraits from an "In between time"'. '*Zwischenzeit*', however, suggests more than simply time in-between, but also in-between place, politics and people. The East

An all-female medical practice in East Berlin

German photographer, Konrad Hoffmeister, had asked his subjects what 'Germany' meant to them, and all the photos were of identical format, one or two people facing the camera, holding a placard summarising their hopes for and thoughts about 'Germany'. The project started in 1985 and covered East and West, people of all ages and walks of life. But all hundred or so photographs were of pure lily-white Germans: there was not one southern European or middle eastern face, let alone anyone of more distant origin. Nor was there any comment on this absence. A strange way to pose the question of German identity, the new beginnings and all that. Some placards, however, made up for the glaring omission, in sentiment at least. Many teenagers voiced fears of renewed German 'arrogance', and the hope that in a reunited Germany racism could be eradicated once and for all. Older people looked forward to Germany being unified but worried about inequality and difference between East and West. 'Tolerance' and 'understanding' were much used words. Some East Germans were sad: they were happy with their old way of life, their placards said, and did not want to lose all they had fought and worked for; there was no need for everything to be turned upside down.

How could old German ethnicity, past anti-semitism, the Holocaust, the new racisms, and new race-blinkers, be reconciled in any new national identity? Such questions must be high on the political agenda for the new/old greater Germany, yet this exhibition was the only explicit reference to German-ness I came across. Odd, that there seems to be much more overt debate about nations and nationalism and national identity in the UK. Concepts like post-coloniality and hybridity are relatively commonplace. Apart from former Yugoslavia, though, most countries discussed are distant from Europe: South Africa in the post-apartheid era, Australia's reorientation to its Pacific region, and the re/building of nationhood in other parts of the former British Empire. The new ways of thinking are scarcely addressed to Germany, despite its crucial location within 'our' region. Here we seem to have only the ranting of the tabloids.

Mine was a short trip. Perhaps I had missed something? Or does the ghost, or fear of the ghost, of the Third Reich still make it too difficult to think of the German nation in the late 1990s in terms which do not recall the ethnic basis of German nationalism of the 1930s, its expansionism, and racial supremacism? Surely not. But I remain puzzled, suspecting that this apparent silence connects somehow with unwillingness to acknowledge 'foreigners' as German.

Perhaps 'national identity' is beside the point. Creating the conditions in which all people can feel themselves to be 'at home' in Germany, a reformulation of citizenship, would provide a more solid foundation than appeals to a shared ethnic or territorial past. In Berlin last summer national or ethnic identity was the last thing I was looking for, or found, and I came away feeling more strongly than ever the absence of a need to possess one.

It was a reckoning, a reconnoitring, not a reconciling. As my mother said, it was the wrong flat. It had to be. The present never meets the past.

Thanks to Ann Curthoys and John Docker for suggesting I write up my Berlin experience.

One day last summer

David Gibson

'I love you all', said Nelson Mandela from the balcony of South Africa House. A sense of wonder and history that day, for here was probably one of the truly great men of this century. All those years of quiet dignity and and patience, and now the joy of sharing his freedom with ordinary people everywhere he goes.

Our next theme issue, *Soundings* No. 7, is *States of Africa* edited by Victoria Brittain and including:
  Basil Davidson
  Rakiya Omaar
  Ngugi wa Mirie
  Kevin Watson
  Joe Hanlon
  Tanzania's Official Report on Corruption,
  with photos by Jenny Mathews.

The price of equality

Affirmative action in the United States

Joanne Barkan

Here is a political puzzle - a sort of philosophical brain-tease - which Americans must learn to solve. It concerns 'affirmative action', meaning all the government and private-sector policies designed to create more opportunities for minorities and women. (Of course, as European societies grow ever more diverse, this puzzle might begin to look less and less like a typically American problem.)

Imagine a prestigious state university - call it Super U - somewhere in the United States. Super U's graduates get the best jobs, so the most successful high-school students in the state want to go there. Super U has places for only one quarter of the applicants and selects those with the finest academic records. Its students are mostly white and Asian American, although citizens of the state include quite a few blacks, Latinos, and Native Americans. Super U claims to want to increase enrolment for these last three groups whose members often live in neighbourhoods with less adequate schools and more social problems. On average, they have lower family incomes.

Now decide this: Which of the following young women deserves the one remaining place in the next freshman class? Susan has worked hard for years, hoping to attend Super U. She has the best academic record and is white. Alice, black, has an acceptable record. Her grandparents and parents didn't have enough money to stay in school; anyway, Super U took practically no black students in those years. Maria has a better academic record than Alice and is the US-born daughter of Nicaraguans. Her wealthy parents immigrated to the United States just before she was born. Ann, a Native American, has slightly lower grades than Alice. She grew up on a poverty-stricken tribal reservation. Her ancestors lived for centuries on the land where Super U now stands.

You should, in theory, find your answer in the principles of liberal democracy. All citizens have equal rights under the law, including equal opportunity to pursue satisfaction and acquire property. Everyone competes on the same playing field; whoever plays the best, wins. Americans have always understood their individual lives, their children's future, and their national history (and its cruel failures) in these terms, which define a meritocracy. Therefore Susan wins the place at Super U.

This clear-cut answer is obviously not correct because Susan, Alice, Maria, and Ann are not playing on a level field. After 350 years of black slavery followed by ninety years of apartheid, after expropriation of the Native Americans who survived genocide, US citizens do not all have equal opportunity. Yet acknowledging this fact (as most Americans do) will not solve the puzzle. The decision to repair the playing field - which is a moral and political imperative - doesn't provide the answer either. It turns out that a meritocracy has no rules for *how* to level an uneven playing field or how to pick the winners while the repair work goes on. No matter which of the four women goes to Super U, someone gets treated unfairly.

So far, the puzzle clarifies the basic structure of the dilemma but nothing of the complexities or scope. Not only is the United States the world's most racially and ethnically diverse society; it has the most unequal distribution of wealth of any prosperous nation, and the shoddiest 'safety net' for the poor. Moreover, like every other liberal democracy, it has denied women full equality of opportunity. Who should go to Super U if Susan's mother is an unemployed widow? Or what if only one of Alice's parents is black? One grandparent? Or what if both parents are black and wealthy? What if they're poor but Alice attended a fine, private high school on scholarship? What if Marie's parents are poor? What if Ann is a young man, and Super U needs to admit more women?

Put aside for a moment the unresolved student dilemmas. How should Super U hire professors? Should the job in the all-male, almost all-white physics department go to the *most* qualified candidate or to one of the fully qualified candidates who is female? A white female or a black male?

Now consider a more general issue. Let's say, for the sake of argument, that Super U has never discriminated against women, blacks, Latinos, or Native Americans when hiring professors. The lack of diversity just happened as the university went about its business in a principled way. Does Super U have an obligation to change the composition of its teaching staff? Is diversity in itself an important - or legitimate - goal for a meritocracy? If so, should the composition of the teaching staff reflect the composition of the appropriate labour pool? Or the student population? Or the state's population?

These questions come up in the United States not as philosophical brain-teasers but as daily policy matters at every educational institution receiving even minimal public funds. And education is only one part of the story. Over the last thirty years, hiring throughout the private and public sectors, job promotions, government contracting to private companies, and racial-ethnic distribution within voting districts, have all come under scrutiny. How much of the economy does this affect? Look at government contracts. According to the Labor Department, 95,000 enterprises, employing 27 million people, share 185 billion dollars in one year.

The 1960s and 1970s

The term 'affirmative action' first appeared in a 1961 executive order, which President John Kennedy signed under pressure from the black civil rights movement. Kennedy ordered employers with federal government contracts to 'take affirmative action' to ensure they didn't discriminate against anyone because of race, religion, colour, or national origin in hiring or on the job. This seemingly small step was the most significant anti-discrimination action taken by a US president in the twentieth century. After all, the Supreme Court hadn't declared government-sanctioned racial segregation unconstitutional until 1954.

In 1964, Congress finally took a stand. It passed the Civil Rights Act which prohibited discrimination because of race, colour, religion, sex, or national origin. Legislators from the South and other conservatives blocked the law until it included language prohibiting preferential treatment for the victims of discrimination. This meant Congress defined the process of levelling the playing field as simply dropping barriers to individual freedom. Members of aggrieved groups would get neither restitution nor special help.

As President Lyndon Johnson signed the legislation, he and civil rights leaders knew that dropping barriers would help only those relatively few individuals who had enough education, skills, and experience to compete successfully. Most blacks (blacks were the focus of concern at the time) would be left where they were - isolated in dire hardship. So almost immediately, Johnson began redefining what it meant to level the playing field. In a 1965 speech at traditionally black Howard University in Washington DC, he offered his now famous sports metaphor:

> You do not take a person who, for years, has been hobbled by chains and liberate him, bring him to the starting line of a race and then say, 'You are free to compete with all the others' and still justly believe you have been completely fair.

Here Johnson articulated what would become the fundamental justification for a new kind of affirmative action - one that would give preferential treatment to members of disadvantaged groups. The federal government would see that blacks got into entry-level jobs, training programmes, and schools. What if they did not score as well on entrance exams? With affirmative action, they would get a 'thumb on the scale', an initial boost.

Most civil rights leaders ended up supporting affirmative action, but some had qualms. They could foresee pitfalls which were moral, social, political, and psychological. First, preferences had the paradoxical moral fault of using racial bias in a new way to correct damage done by the old bias. Instead of creating a 'race-neutral' playing field, preferences skewed some (but by no means all) rules in favour of blacks.

Second, the new rules would probably generate white resentment and aggravate social tensions - as had every other effort of blacks to achieve equality. Affirmative action would, in fact, put the most vulnerable nonblacks at greater risk unless the economy continuously produced more jobs and bigger schools. If the economy stagnated - or even if it didn't expand fast enough - conservative politicians would 'play the race card': they would win over poor and working-class whites by blaming these peoples' difficulties on blacks benefitting from affirmative action. Thus the 'natural' constituency of the left would be split. Affirmative action might undermine progressive coalitions, making a progressive majority impossible in the United States.

Finally, sceptics believed race-based preferences posed a psychological risk. They might stigmatise blacks in their own minds. Beneficiaries might always think, 'I wasn't good enough to make it on my own'. Or they might assume others were thinking, 'He'd never have that job if he weren't black'.

Despite these misgivings, supporters of affirmative action believed they could defend the policy in a principled way. Supreme Court Justice Harry Blackmun summed up their position when he wrote later on, 'In order to get beyond racism, we must first take account of race'. The argument presumed preferences would not last forever. Once they had repaired the damage from past discrimination, they would be dropped in favour of meritocracy. Some affirmative action supporters also pointed out that rescuing the American meritocracy amounted to salvaging a myth. Given the influence of money, social connections, nepotism, and regional differences, the United States had never been a meritocracy.

In the 1960s, most civil rights leaders saw race-based preferences as a supplemental tool at best. After passage of the Civil Rights Act, the strategy of Dr Martin Luther King and allies focused on reshaping the US economy. The goal was equality of opportunity for all Americans. Like the rest of the democratic left, they wanted full employment, skills training, good public schools, national health care, decent housing, affordable child care, and drug prevention for everyone. They did not deny the existence of racism autonomous of economic issues; if the best-qualified candidates were black, they still might not get the jobs simply because of prejudice. But radical economic reform combined with rigorous enforcement of the new civil rights law seemed to add up to substantial equality of opportunity.

Lyndon Johnson backed the call for more opportunities for low-income Americans; they - black and white - were a key Democratic Party constituency. He launched his Great Society economic and social programmes in 1965. The escalating war in Vietnam, however, undermined Johnson politically. It also devoured tremendous amounts of revenue and set off inflation, rocking the economy. Measured against what Johnson's War on Poverty realistically needed, resources shrivelled up. Some good came out of the programmes, but ultimately the effort was too limited, too short-lived, and perhaps too centralised to solve multiplying problems.

In the meantime, the federal government doggedly pursued affirmative action in contracting, employment, and education. Racial preferences had the great advantage of speeding up the integration process by forcing all-white businesses, schools, and government departments to adopt ongoing programmes. Year by year, the definition of affirmative action evolved as the government tried new procedures, always pushing against the limits established in the Civil Rights Act. The ability to disperse funds gave the federal government leverage over state and local governments and the private sector.

In 1966, the Labor Department began asking companies to submit affirmative action plans for minority hiring *before* they bid on construction contracts. By 1968, all government contracts required plans with goals and timetables. In 1969, Republican Richard Nixon became President. His administration's Philadelphia Plan for contracting required minority hiring goals set as a percentage of a company's total payroll. As bizarre as it now seems, his appointees pushed affirmative action further than the Johnson administration. Nixon hoped to avert the riots that tore through hundreds of urban ghettos in the 1960s. Most historians also believe that his more Machiavellian purpose was to splinter the Democratic Party's electorate over time.

Nixon's Labor Department took another major step in 1970. It required affirmative action plans whenever the number of black employees was lower than what could be 'reasonably expected' given their availability. The roster of workers had to reflect the local labour pool even when a company had not discriminated intentionally. The government thus confirmed diversity - and not just repair of past discrimination - as an affirmative action goal. (In 1978, the Carter administration went further when it defined 'reasonably expected' numerically as four-fifths the selection rate of the racial group with the highest selection rate.) In 1971, the Labor Department extended affirmative action to women. Then Latinos, Asian Americans, Native Americans, and Alaskan native tribes were added. In 1979, Congress voted to reserve 10 per cent of government contracts for minority-owned businesses.

This type of affirmative action broke open 'lily-white' and 'old-boy' enclaves in American society. Many fire departments and police departments hired nonwhites and women for the first time. The steelworkers' union, the construction unions, and other all-white unions with control over skilled trades were forced to integrate. Major corporations such as AT&T had to reform their rigid caste systems which kept nonwhites and women in lower-wage jobs. The universities came under pressure to diversify their populations. Nonwhites and women slowly entered all-white, all-male law firms, hospital administrations, news rooms, research laboratories, foundations, and publishing houses. The tiny black middle class grew.

Opponents challenged affirmative action in the law courts every step of the way. White men, seeing their favoured position in society under assault, protested on the grounds of 'reverse discrimination'. Institutions, no longer free to set all their own rules, resisted. In addition, everyone needed clarification. What was the difference in practice between a lawful 'goal' for minority hiring and an unlawful racial quota system? Did identical rules govern both the public and private sectors? Did affirmative action apply to layoffs as well as to hiring?

'Most historians believe that Nixon's more Machiavellian purpose was to splinter the Democratic Party's electorate'

The US Supreme Court decided no less than seventeen significant affirmative action cases over twenty-five years. Unfortunately, the decisions do not add up to a logically developed sequence of interpretation. Some decisions completely reverse others; all are ambiguous or incomplete. The pattern since 1978, however, is growing opposition to setting aside a fixed number of places for a particular group. The Court has rejected using race as the sole criterion for selection although race as one of several factors still qualifies. The Court also seemed to accept diversity (along with remedying past discrimination) as a legitimate goal. But after some recent confusing decisions in lower courts, no one really knows what kind of affirmative action programmes are legal.

Thinking practically, could there ever be one set of rules for, say, the Kaiser Aluminum Corporation, the Miami Fire Department, and Stanford University? Unlike early civil rights disputes over American apartheid, affirmative action defies a one-shot solution. Saying 'no' to the whites-only drinking fountain or to blacks being forced to ride at the back of the bus required simply 'doing the right thing'. Doing the right thing with affirmative action is far more complex.

The Supreme Court has also swayed with shifting political winds in the United States. The backlash against affirmative action helped to elect Ronald Reagan president in 1980. Reagan, who opposed both the 1964 Civil Rights Act and the

1965 Voting Rights Act, replaced retiring Supreme Court justices with conservatives whom he knew would undo affirmative action.

(An ironic note from the annals of civil rights history: Reagan named Clarence Thomas to run the Equal Employment Opportunity Commission, which John Kennedy had established in his 1961 executive order. Thomas was a young black lawyer who had converted from affirmative-action beneficiary to die-hard opponent. In 1991, George Bush nominated Thomas to the Supreme Court. His nomination ran into trouble when a former EEOC employee accused him of sexual harassment. Thomas nonetheless made it onto the Court where he consistently votes against affirmative action.)

Wedge issues?

History since 1965 has confirmed the early fears of civil rights advocates. For some folks, affirmative action does pose the stigmatising question, 'Could I (you) have made it without special help?' As time goes by, some supporters of affirmative action are increasingly uncomfortable with the moral dilemma. How long will it take to level the playing field? Will we ever become a society that looks beyond race and gender, that is 'neutral' because it is truly fair? Some leftists worry that the left's own promotion of racial, ethnic, cultural, and gender differences and 'identity politics' has divided the United States further. For many, all the counting and labelling ('Put Judy on the Native American list because one of her great-grandfathers was a Cherokee') have become odious.

No affirmative action dilemma weighs more heavily on the left than the political one. Republican party strategists have used race and gender shamelessly - and effectively - since the 1960s to sabotage progressive politics. They fuelled the fears of working-class and lower-middle-class whites about job competition, crime, and the end of traditional family life. They wanted voters to see the Democratic party as the home of job-stealing minorities and men-hating women who demanded special treatment, who would not play by the rules, who relied on 'left-leaning' big government.

Richard Nixon used these 'wedge issues' in his famous 'southern strategy' for the Republican Party to win over southern and southwestern whites. The strategy worked. The Republicans are now the majority party in those regions, which gives them an overall advantage in presidential races and in winning a congressional majority. Some political commentators argue that as long as affirmative action exists, progressives will never again assemble a majority.

The era of affirmative action coincides with the long-term restructuring of the US economy and loss of global hegemony. The disappearance of good-paying manufacturing jobs, the near demise of labour unions in the private sector (less than 11 per cent of workers belong), the stagnation of middle- and working-class wages, structural unemployment, 'downsizing' in successful companies (that is, reducing the number of employees to raise short-term profit margins), the growing disparity between the very rich and everyone else - these describe the trajectory of the US economy over the last twenty-five years.

The best alternative to affirmative action - Martin Luther King's dream of a dynamic, democratised economy - never materialised. In the unfavourable context since the early 1970s, affirmative action has been a weak, flawed tool for repairing the damage of discrimination. Yet one shudders to think what American society would look like without it.

The US left has staunchly defended affirmative action - to the point, some say, of creating a sacred cow: *Thou shalt not question affirmative action on pain of losing your left credentials.* But a few voices - nonwhite and white - wonder aloud whether the liabilities now outweigh the benefits. Some suggest replacing racial, ethnic, and gender preferences with class-based affirmative action. People who have suffered economic and social disadvantages would get a 'thumb on the scale' for entry-level jobs and schooling. Presumably strict enforcement of anti-discrimination laws would protect individuals from racial and gender prejudice.

Class-based affirmative action received a flurry of attention a year or so ago from conservatives as well as centrists and a few progressives. Yet it looks like a messy business which might not resolve any problems. Low-income whites consistently score higher than low-income blacks on university admission tests. So simple economic affirmative action would end up resegregating sought-after schools. Moreover, it wouldn't help women to enter, say, the carpenters' union. And consider a high school administration looking for a new maths teacher. When interviewing several graduates of Columbia University's Teachers College, why would it make sense to give preference to the applicant whose family has a lower income?

Once again, these questions are not hypothetical. In July 1995, the governing board of the vast University of California banned race, religion, sex, colour, ethnicity, and national origin as criteria for employment, student admission, and contracting.

When university administrators opposed the change, the board told them to use criteria such as 'difficult family situation' and economic disadvantage when choosing between student applicants in the special preference pool (all applicants must meet the minimum academic requirements).

'Visible to the naked eye is a society in which women, blacks, and some other minorities, are not equal players'

So who gets into prestigious UC Berkeley? The kid whose difficult family situation includes a drug-pusher father in prison or the kid whose brother died in a drive-by shooting and whose mother has multiple sclerosis? The category of economic disadvantage gets equally convoluted because sociologists want to distinguish between the long-term poor and the supposedly less-deserving 'newly poor' (for example, those who lost jobs when defence plants and army bases closed in recent years). But exactly how does an unemployed engineer who is becoming an alcoholic stack up against the single mother who does cleaning in a nursing home? Suppose the engineer's wife asks for a divorce. Suppose she attempts suicide. Meanwhile conservatives always complain that race- and gender-based affirmative action encourages citizens to compete over 'victim status'.

Look around the United States today to see who works where, who earns what, and who studies for how long. Visible to the naked eye is a society in which women, blacks, and some other minorities are not equal players. The work of integrating the upper echelons has barely begun. Some 95 per cent of the highest executive jobs in corporate America belong to white men. Last year, a federal court banned an affirmative action programme at the University of Texas Law School because it set lower standards for minority applicants. The programme had raised the Latino presence in the 1992 entering class to 10.7 per cent. Yet Texas has a Latino population of 25.6 percent. Without affirmative action, school administrators expect the 1998 class to be all white.

So the United States still needs some kind of affirmative action; at the same time, affirmative action needs more consistently democratic management. More of the people who live with the programmes should help to design and monitor them. This is not a quixotic scheme. In the real world, many reasonable employers and employees set up successful training programmes years ago. Many reasonable school administrators and students agreed on effective hiring and admissions plans. Berkeley's banned admissions policy, for example, worked well by most accounts. Apparently we are not reasonable enough right now to continue down this road. On 5 November 1996, Californians voted on a referendum to ban race, sex, colour, ethnicity, and national origin as criteria in *all* public employment, education, and contracting. The measure passed by a large margin. As opponents challenge the California law in court, other states are planning similar referenda.

Addressing insecurity

Affirmative action will lose the popular vote as long as too many middle- and working-class Americans feel insecure about today's jobs and tomorrow's standard of living; they resent, or fear, giving 'a leg up' to 'special groups'. Of course, they have reason to feel insecure. The weak public sector has never provided for the general welfare. Even the niggardly safety net for Americans in trouble has been slashed back. In the private sector, employers use the global economy with its low-wage workers in Thailand and Mexico as a bludgeon to beat back wage demands. Although the official unemployment rate has fallen below 6 per cent, millions of Americans still don't have jobs or they work hard for less than a living wage.

How should the left in 1997 propose creating substantial equality of opportunity in the United States? What policies will win political support? First, we need economic growth stronger than the average 2 + per cent characteristic of the last several years. This will require a Federal Reserve Board less beholden to deflation-loving bankers and financial markets. Second, the government needs to use tax incentives, to direct economic growth into job creation rather than stock market speculation and luxury consumption. (When former Labor Secretary Robert Reich proposed this in 1995, Treasury Secretary Robert Rubin got the White House to nix all such notions.) Third, new jobs in a growing economy have to pay better wages. This presupposes nothing less than a revived labour movement. (Most left economists agree that lower unemployment in the United States has not translated into better wages because the unions are so feeble.)

A dynamic jobs-oriented economy creates the only possibility of building an adequate public sector in the United States. Welfare provision (unemployment and disability insurance, old-age pensions, health insurance, food and rent subsidies), labour market policies (training, job placement, relocation, temporary public-sector work), and infrastructure in the broad sense (schools at every level, libraries, child care, transportation systems, research facilities, environmental repair and protection) require lots of money - tax money. Americans - tax phobic since prerevolutionary times - may never come around to financing an adequate public sector. They won't, however, even turn in that direction until they feel more economically secure and until the tax system is less regressive.

There's the programme. In the best of all worlds - let's say, Martin Luther King Jr.'s world—our radically reformed economy and energetically implemented civil rights laws would create equal opportunity. We would need affirmative action programmes only to integrate whatever schools and work places remained closed. We would stop weighing disadvantages and totalling up ethnicities...we would...

Hopelessly utopian, no doubt. But like other valuable utopian schemes (those aimed at more democracy and liberty as well as social justice), the vision provides some concrete ideas about tactics on the ground. The left should defend successful affirmative action programmes but realise that levelling the playing field requires more ample and radical plans.

The medicalisation of modern living

Joanna Moncrieff

Joanna Moncrieff argues that psychiatry is a disguised form of social control which, despite a history of resistance, is currently increasing its power.

The institution of psychiatry grew up in the nineteenth century during the emergence and consolidation of industrial capitalism. Its function was to deal with abnormal and bizarre behaviour which, without breaking the law, did not comply with the demands of the new social and economic order. Its association with medicine concealed this political function of social control, by endowing it with the objectivity and neutrality of science. The medical model of mental disorder has served ever since to obscure the social processes that produce and define deviance by locating problems in individual biology. This obfuscation lends itself to the perpetuation of the established order, by side-stepping the challenge that is implicit in deviant behaviour and thereby undermining a source of criticism and opposition. During the twentieth century, a fierce attack on psychiatry has condemned this misleading medical characterisation of the problems of living, and the repressive measures that masquerade as psychiatric treatment. However, at the same time, more sophisticated technology has enabled the psychiatric profession not only to weather the storm, but to strengthen its claim to the jurisdiction of 'mental illness'. Opportunities for social control and the suppression of dissent in the guise of psychiatry have increased.

In some respects psychiatry has never been as confident and respectable as it is at present. In the 1950s and 1960s a pharmacological revolution produced an array of drugs for use in disorders such as schizophrenia, depression and anxiety, which enabled psychiatry to move closer to the paradigm of physical medicine, of administering specific cures for specific conditions. Starting in this period also, psychiatric care relocated physically, away from the discredited asylums and into general hospitals, in closer proximity to the rest of the medical community. This move embodied the attempts of the psychiatric profession to disentangle itself from the stigma of caring for the chronically insane, and instead to forge a role curing the acutely disturbed. Community care is the concession to the chronic and recurrent nature of psychiatric conditions.

Similarly, the endeavour to locate the biological origins of mental illness has been revitalised by the introduction of new technology for studying the brain, and by the development of molecular genetics and the human genome project. Despite a disappointing lack of consistent results, the quantity of resources devoted to this research has, in itself, leant the medical model of mental illness further credibility.

However, the twentieth century has also produced an influential critique of psychiatry articulated by academics and some rebel psychiatrists (famously, R.D. Laing, Thomas Szasz and David Cooper). Sociological theories of deviance, medicalisation and the organisation of professions helped to expose the political functions and processes involved in the institution of psychiatry. The paternalism of psychiatry was attacked and medical treatment was accused of being more oppressive than legal sanctions or punishment.

These ideas were expressed in concrete form in the activities of protest movements, patient advocacy groups and experiments in alternative care. In the early 1970s in the Netherlands and the United States, where protest movements were particularly strong, there were demonstrations against the use of electro convulsive therapy (ECT), university lectures were disrupted and some prominent biological psychiatrists had to have police protection. There were famous attempts to create therapeutic communities which renounced staff/patient distinctions and hierarchies (such as R.D. Laing's Kingsley Hall and David Cooper's Ward 21 in the United Kingdom); and in Italy a politically conscious democratic psychiatry movement instituted mental health care reforms. The patient advocacy movement, which took inspiration from civil rights organisations, was another important development. Although the activism has diminished, patient or survivor groups remain strong, and individuals and groups of professionals continue to promote alternative approaches to the problems of the so-called mentally ill. The 'antipsychiatry' movement also had a significant impact on social policy, resulting in increasing restrictions on involuntary confinement and treatment, and a diminishing use of physical techniques such as psychosurgery and ECT.

However, recent developments in the definition and management of two major psychiatric conditions, depression and schizophrenia, illustrate that the social influence and formal powers of institutional psychiatry may now be expanding. The criticism that was first expressed over three decades ago may therefore be more relevant than ever.

Depression: medicalising discontent

The Defeat Depression Campaign (DDC), launched in 1992, was organised by the Royal College of Psychiatrists in association with the Royal College of General Practitioners with funding from the pharmaceutical industry. The literature of this campaign suggests that around 10 per cent of the population suffer from a depressive disorder at any one time, a third will suffer at some time during their lives, and antidepressant drugs are recommended for all those with moderate to severe symptoms. These claims seem to suggest that a large proportion of human unhappiness is biologically based and can be similarly corrected. The publicity surrounding the new antidepressant fluoxetine (prozac) has become only slightly more extreme, with claims that it has personality altering and general life enhancing properties.[1]

A recent collection of interviews with prominent psychopharmacologists who were involved with the discovery and introduction of modern psychiatric drugs provides an interesting historical backdrop to the DDC.[2] In psychiatric hospital practice in the 1950s depression was a relatively rare disorder and there was no concept of a specifically antidepressant drug, as opposed to a general stimulant.

1. See P.D. Kramer, *Listening to prozac. A psychiatrist explores antidepressant drugs and the remaking of the self*, Viking, New York, 1993.
2. *The psychopharmacologists. Interviews by Dr. David Healy*, Chapman & Hall, London 1996.

When the antidepressant action of certain compounds was first proposed, drug companies were initially reluctant to develop and launch such drugs. In an unconscious alliance of interests, influential psychiatrists developed and popularised the view of depression as a common biologically based disorder, amenable to drug treatment and as yet frequently unrecognised.[3] This concept had the dual benefits of vastly expanding the market for psychiatric drugs and extending the boundaries of psychiatry outside the asylum. Since this time, the psychiatric profession and the drug industry have continued to try and inculcate this idea into the consciousness of both the general public and other doctors. The DDC is the latest offensive.

Numerous biochemical mechanisms responsible for depressive illness have been proposed implicating a variety of biochemical and hormonal mechanisms, partly determined by fashion. The evidence for all these theories has been inconsistent, but the consensus about the efficacy of antidepressant drugs remains the strongest support for the thesis that depression is a physiological condition. Perusing the psychiatric literature indicates that this consensus developed in the mid 1970s, based on evidence from randomised controlled trials of the original and still widely used antidepressants, the tricyclics. However, early reviews of this evidence portray an ambiguous situation with a large proportion of trials failing to find a positive effect.[4] In addition, more recently some researchers have suggested that antidepressants are not specifically active against depression but merely exert a placebo effect in a receptive condition.[5] They appear to perform better than an inert placebo because their side effects increase their suggestive power, and they may also admit bias into the assessment procedure by enabling investigators to guess whether patients are on the active drug or the placebo. A recent meta-analysis of placebo controlled trials of prozac found that the likelihood of recovery was indeed

3. See F.J. Ayd, *Recognising the depressed patient*, Grune & Stratton, New York 1961.
4. For example A. Smith, E. Traganza & G. Harrison, 'Studies on the effectiveness of antidepressant drugs', *Psychopharmacology* (supplement), 1-53, 1969; and J.B. Morris & A. Beck, 'The efficacy of antidepressant drugs. A review of research (1958 to 1972)' *Archives of General Psychiatry* 30, 667-674, 1974.
5. R.P. Greenberg & S. Fisher, 'Examining antidepressant effectiveness: findings, ambiguities and some vexing puzzles', chap 1, pp1-39 in *The limits of biological treatments for psychological distress*, editors S. Fisher & R.P. Greenberg, Lawrence Erlbaum Associates, Hillsdale, New Jersey, 1989.

associated with experiencing side effects.[6] A review of seven studies which used an active substance as a placebo to mimic antidepressant side effects found that only one showed the drug to be superior.[7]

Variation in mood is a characteristically human way of responding to circumstances but unhappiness has become taboo in the late twentieth century, perhaps because it undermines the image that society wishes to project. Medicalisation diminishes the legitimacy of grief and discontent, and therefore reduces the repertoire of acceptable human responses to events and denies people the opportunity to indulge their feelings. At the same time it diverts attention away from the

> 'There has developed a view of depression as a common biologically based disorder, amenable to drug treatment'

political and environmental factors that can make modern life so difficult and distressing. It may be no coincidence that the concept of depression has reached its present peak of popularity in western societies reeling from two decades of increased unemployment and the marginalisation of a substantial section of the population.

However, it is also important to acknowledge that people have different propensities to experience intense moods and that, for those at the extremes of this spectrum, such as those with manic depressive disorder, life can be very difficult. Prophylactic medication is promoted by psychiatrists for long-term use in this condition primarily in the form of lithium. However, in a similar way to antidepressants, claims of the efficacy of lithium seem to have been based on insubstantial evidence and follow-up studies of people with manic depression do not indicate that it has improved the outlook of the condition.[8] It is possible therefore that prophylactic drug treatment constitutes a false hope held out to people who feel

---

6. R.P. Greenberg, R.F. Bornstein, M.J. Zborowski, S. Fisher & M.D. Greenberg. 'A meta-analysis of fluoxetine outcome in the treatment of depression', *Journal of Nervous and Mental Disease* 182, 547-551, 1994; R. Thomson. 'Side effects and placebo amplification', *British Journal of Psychiatry* 140, 64-68, 1982.
7. R. Thomson, 'Side effects and placebo amplification,' *British Journal of Psychiatry* 140, 64-68, 1982.
8. J. Moncrieff, '"Lithium revisited". A re-examination of the placebo-controlled trials of lithium prophylaxis in manic-depressive disorder', *British Journal of Psychiatry* 167, 569-573, 1995.

desperate, by a profession that feels helpless. It may serve only further to undermine the self assurance of people who are already vulnerable. For such people, instead of aspiring to complete cure, natural remission of episodes should be encouraged by providing care and security; and attempts should be made to enhance people's confidence in their own ability to manage or survive their condition.

Schizophrenia: disguising social control

The enormous investment in the investigation of the biological basis of schizophrenia has produced no conclusive information. Decades of increasingly sophisticated technological research has revealed a possible weak genetic predisposition, often much exaggerated by psychiatric commentators who ignore the shortcomings of the main studies.[9] Molecular genetic studies have publicised initial findings implicating several different genes which then transpired to be due to chance when attempts at replication failed. The most recent pan-European study boldly concludes that the genetic associations revealed are involved in the pathogenesis of the disorder. However, the gene implicated is common in the general population; it is only slightly more common in people diagnosed with schizophrenia and the similarity of the comparison group in this study was ensured only for ethnicity and not for other factors.[10] As regards brain function and anatomy, the only consistent finding is the larger size of the lateral ventricle, one of the brain cavities, in people with schizophrenia. Again there is a substantial overlap with the 'normal' population, and most studies have been conducted on people with long histories of drug treatment. However, the possibility that drugs may be responsible for causing the brain abnormalities observed has received little attention in the psychiatric literature.[11]

---

9. S. Rose, R.C. Lewontin and L.J. Kamin, *Not in our genes*, Penguin Books, London 1984.
10. J. Williams, G. Spurlock, P. McGuffin, J. Mallet, M.M. Nothen, M Gill, H. Aschauer, P. Nylander, F. Macciardi and M.J. Owen. 'Association between schizophrenia and T102C polymorphism of the 5-hydroxytryptamine type 2a-receptor gene', *Lancet* 347, 1294-1296, 1996.
11. A recent review by S.E. Chua & P.J. McKenna 'Schizophrenia-a brain disease? A critical review of structural and functional cerebral abnormality in the disorder' in the *British Journal of Psychiatry* 166, 563-582, 1995, fails to consider the confounding effects of drug treatment. P. Breggin reviews the evidence of an association between drug treatment and brain abnormalities, in 'Brain damage, dementia and persistent cognitive dysfunction associated with neuroleptic drugs: evidence, etiology and implications', *Journal of Mind and Behavior* 11, 425-63, 1990.

Drugs variously termed 'major tranquillisers,' 'neuroleptics' or 'antipsychotics' form the mainstay of psychiatric treatment for schizophrenia. They have been claimed to have specific action against psychotic symptoms such as delusions and hallucinations, but critics suggest that they act in a much cruder way by producing a chemical lobotomy or straitjacket which inhibits all creative thought processes.[12] Psychiatry applauds the role of these drugs in emptying the asylums but an alternative perspective suggests that they merely helped to replace expensive custodial care with long-term drug-induced control.[13]

A consequence of the move towards community care is that public and political anxiety has replaced the concern for patients' rights with concern for protection of the community and psychiatric treatment has become the panacea for this complex social problem. In response to a few highly publicised cases of violent or dangerous acts by former psychiatric patients, amendments were made to the Mental Health Act (1983), which came into force in April 1996 and which introduce a power of 'supervised discharge'. This power enables psychiatric personnel to have access to the patient if deemed necessary and to enforce attendance at psychiatric facilities. It does not confer the right to enforce medical treatment but it does require that an assessment for admission to hospital be conducted if the patient is uncompliant with aftercare arrangements such as refusing medication. The justification for this legislation is the assumption that medical treatment can cure disturbance and prevent relapse. However the evidence indicates that a substantial proportion of people with a psychotic episode fail to respond to medication at all, that a further significant proportion relapse despite taking long-term medication (in clinical trials the relapse rate on medication is around 30 per cent) and, like other people, they may behave antisocially when they are not actively psychotic.

The social control element of the changes to the Mental Health Act is only thinly veiled and they have been strongly opposed by civil and patients' rights groups. Their significance lies in the introduction of a new precedent, of control over people after discharge from hospital. The use of the former 1983 Mental Health Act for these purposes was successfully challenged in the courts in the 1980s. The

---

12 P. Breggin, *Toxic psychiatry*, Fontana, London 1993.
13. A. Scull, 'Deinstitutionalisation: cycles of despair', *Journal of Mind and Behavior* 11, 301-312, 1990; and T. Szasz, *Cruel compassion*, John Wiley & Sons, New York 1994.

exact form of the new provisions when implemented is uncertain and is likely to vary according to the predisposition of local professionals. Although there is much unease among psychiatrists about shouldering increased responsibility for the actions of people labelled mentally ill, many in the profession have called for stronger powers to enforce medical treatment in the community.

The medical model of mental illness has facilitated the move towards greater restriction, by cloaking it under the mantle of treatment. This process of medicalisation of deviant behaviour conceals complex political issues about the tolerance of diversity, the control of disruptive behaviour and the management of dependency. It enables a society that professes liberal values and individualism to impose and re-inforce conformity. It disguises the economics of a system in which human labour is valued only for the profit it can generate, marginalising all those who are not fit or not willing to be so exploited.

Characterisation of schizophrenia as a physically based disease of the brain also forecloses any debate about the meaning of the experiences and actions associated with it. Attempts to render schizophrenic symptoms intelligible and to understand their communicative value help both to illuminate ordinary experience and to increase empathy for people with this condition.[14] Other interesting findings point to the association of schizophrenia with features of social structure. Nothing resembling schizophrenia was described prior to the early nineteenth century, suggesting an association with the emergence of industrial capitalism. In modern societies schizophrenia is more frequently diagnosed in urban centres, and among people of lower social class; it is also more common in certain immigrant groups than in people of their country of origin, particularly in second generation Afro-Caribbean people in the UK. Research in the third world has shown that people there with schizophrenia have a better prognosis, with a lower chance of relapse and functional decline than their counterparts in the industrial world.[15] It appears therefore that social conditions play a part in determining the expression of schizophrenic symptoms and so schizophrenia may be regarded as a mirror on the

---

14. Examples are R.D. Laing, *The Divided Self*, Pelican Books, London 1965; and more recently, L.A. Sass, *The Paradoxes of Delusion: Wittgenstein, Schreber and the Schizophrenic Mind*, Cornell University Press, Ithaca 1994.
15. This research, as well as evidence on other structural factors, is reviewed in R. Warner, *Recovery from schizophrenia: psychiatry and political economy*, Routledge & Kegan Paul, London 1985.

deficiencies of the current social structure.

Tolerance of the diversity of human lives and a respect for the autonomy of all must be the foundation of a progressive alternative approach. Enhancing people's control over their lives means providing genuine choices and opportunities for people of all different propensities. It means creating a society where there are niches available that allow a diversity of lifestyles. It involves accepting that some people may chose to lead lives that appear bizarre or impoverished. Although some people with schizophrenia will find drug treatment useful, psychiatrists' frequent complaints about non-compliance illustrate that many choose not to take medication. Similarly, some people with chronic mental illness gravitate away from the structured, rehabilitating environment of the mental health services to homeless hostels and to the streets. It is commonplace to blame the underfunding of community care for this phenomenon but research has found that most of the psychiatrically ill homeless had not come straight from closing hospitals but had been settled in adequate community accommodation before drifting away.[16] An alternative explanation might be that the long-term mentally ill prefer the undemanding nature of the homeless situation to the intrusive demands of family, community and mental health services.

> 'Nothing resembling schizophrenia was described prior to the early nineteenth century'

The management of disruptive and dangerous behaviour is a problem for every society. Involuntary confinement and treatment continue to be a major area of contention, with opposition, emphasising the need to respect people's autonomy, and opposing the imposition of a relative set of values about what is normal and sane. It is argued that it should be possible to deal with behaviour that is genuinely harming or harassing other people through using normal legal sanctions. This is an area which requires further and wider consideration. Whatever solution is adopted, it must be developed openly and democratically, with proper provision for representation and public scrutiny, so that measures taken can not be subverted to serve the ends of certain groups above others.

---

16. A good review of this area is by J. Scott, 'Homelessness and mental illness', *British Journal of Psychiatry* 162, 314-324, 1993.

Conclusion

Despite the political and professional retrenchment of recent years, there are many developments which presage the ultimate transformation of the psychiatric system. The burgeoning patients' rights movement and the anti-psychiatry critique are some of these. Rejection of paternalism is also embodied in the increasingly important role of consumers in medicine in general, and the demand for justification of treatments and involvement in decision making. The medical profession is also placing more emphasis on objective evidence about the effectiveness of procedures, and showing less inclination to support the principle of clinical freedom. Many individual psychiatrists are aware of the political conflicts that beset their practice, and try to address these thoughtfully and with respect for their patients; and philosophical debate, which inevitably touches on political issues, is flourishing within the profession at present. It is unlikely however that psychiatry will be radically transformed without profound social and political change. The control of deviance and the enforcement of conformity are too central to the smooth functioning of the divisive and exploitative social system in which we live.

Five poems

Epitaphs for Ralph Samuel

Iraqui poets, one room Jews,
strugglers for justice come to rest
in Highgate, with a shared bequest,
welcome this seeker after clues.

He was a scholar, disobedient
to dictate by an epic muse;
so Laws and verdicts were refused
in favour of more telling evidence.

Encyclopede of labour's past,
he had too many books in mind
to get them written down in time;
he stayed impatient, iconoclast.

He took no pride in certainty
but worried Clio's tidy head
with ragged ends and still unread
ambitions for the ordinary.

Let others look for master plans;
he took another path, through archives
tracing silent, unofficial lives,
to bring us news of history's also rans.

continued overleaf

continued from previous page

Under the furrowed gaze of Marx
this Old Mole burrows into richer earth,
stirring the Internationale of death
with local elements, periodic arts.

Beside the sacred plot, ignored,
he'll dig up Griffiths, famous to his wife,
who 'Fell Asleep'; - a dormant life
unsung, untitled, but not unscored.

Epigones beware, there are no lines
to follow, and no legacy but Ralph's
own hope that people might discover faith
in what no epitaph can frame: the times
when change is authored by a thousand hands
and Justice dances in its promised land.

Phil Cohen

I wanted (for Alasdair)

I wanted to lick you
when they wrapped you in my arms
and I saw your bewildered face, still sticky
with streaked, dark blood.
I wanted to clean you with my tongue
flicking laboriously over your bruised features
like a cow with its calf, hot breath
into your ears and nose, washing you
so you could be free of me -

I stopped myself. They cleaned you with water
ridding the stain of birth fluids
from your matted hair.
And weighed and measured you so that
I could have the measure of you.

Into the night they wheeled us
your batting brow battering my breast
swollen and timid in your fierce mouth.
I slipped a furtive tongue across your cheek
and tasted the residue of your waters
where you had swum and struggled until
you broke through; a hot wet exodus
of fluid and blood -

held your hand in one hand and felt
the bruises ripen and deepen along my arms
where the drips had pulsed into my veins.

I wish now I had washed you like the beasts
in the fields, thoroughly and without revulsion.
Lapping you up, while you grunted
Milking me dry

Catherine Smith

Insomnia
after Jeff Wall

He is there again, staring into the space
under the freezer, grease and blackened dust
usual as pillow lace to his blank eyes'

resentful ache, hair of the carpet tiles
edging its way through brushed-cotton pyjamas.
He is like the white

fluorescent tube over the kitchen window,
relentless. If you got close the same
dead-machine hum

would send you screaming. I think he is becoming
smooth as the blue-green eggshell-painted cupboards
beside the sink. His feet

are like the snout of some forest animal,
hairy, and grey, and cold. I think he is
most of himself, like this, at three a.m.,

Foetal beneath the spindly breakfast-table,
listening for spiders, switches, treacheries.

Ruth Valentine

Green Lanes with Skateboarder

The skyline was moody and rough,
everyone heading off towards
their various disappointments,
up Green Lanes in small dull bursts,

when down Green Lanes, a single figure
gliding through the broken straggle
appeared: seraphic, mobile,
an unlikely Visitation

from the lemony morning sky,
flowing past the station beggars
on a secret current, crossing
the slight river's own contra-flow

till at ten yards off it took shape
as a Chinese boy on a skateboard
smiling to his Walkman, removed
from the clog and thwart of traffic.

His drift was smooth, swift as a gull's,
whose single wing flick missed, you gazed
rapt at its infinite cadence.
His face unmarked as the fading moon.

Judy Gahagan

The shaming of the true

Faced with the need to prepare
A kind of balance-sheet
I succumb to the temptation
To exaggerate my faults
And get in first, as at dances
I used to apologise: 'I can do
The quickstep but can't manage the waltz.'
In fact I was no good at either.

Things out of place, not good or bad,
Are the summation of life.
If definitions get to you
You may lose everything - wife,
Talent, humour, constancy.
Shoving words around can hurt,
There are lies of degree,
Father becoming son becoming father.

Eternity will not be eternal enough
To satisfy revenge.
Repentance can't get its tongue
Round the real charge.
Reality is always young.
I would ask a saint if one were at large
How to die peacefully
Among the shouts of when and why and whether.

Peter Porter

A Brief History of Life the University and Everything in 7.9 Chapters

In the beginning was the Word and the Word was Version One Point Zero. And the Word was without form and was sore in need of an acronym. And that acronym should stand for the trinity of Goals, Objectives and Dearing, so Word created GOD.

And on the first day God created the Firmament. But it was despis-ed by the marketing people .'Yeah, verily, this is not a goer' they quoth and 'We seek new income-generation streams, but it produceth them not'.

So on the second day He created the Earth and the early pilot testing results thereof were pleasing unto His eye.

On the third day He created the trees of the forest. But He overdid it a little so on the fourth day He created bureaucracy, Higher Education and, in final desperation, the Open University so that the trees might be kept in thrall.

And the fifth day was a Friday so He decided to take unto Himself a personal research day, which made it into a nice long weekend.

And on the eighth day God said 'Let there be academics'. But they erred in their lectures and strayed from their mission statements like lost sheep, so He also created secretaries and technicians to be their help meets.

Then, just for the Hell of it, God created administrators and managers and other creeping things that creepeth upon the earth. And they went forth and multiplied and began to speak in tongues. And they dwelt in a world that was their own.

And on the ninth day God created those little yellow post-it things, over-head projectors, the Higher Education Funding Council and lots of other really neat stuff.

And on the tenth day He saw everything that He had made and, behold, it was very good.

But on the eleventh day the Four Auditors of the Apocalypse arrived saying 'How knowest Thou that it is "very good"?' and 'Wherefore art Thy performance indicators?' And among the senior managers there was much grinding of teeth, rending of Armani raiment and massaging of data.

And on the great day of reckoning the Auditors
spake in bullet points thus:

Research

♦ We appreciate that peer group assessment is tricky if , as Thou maintain, Thou art the one and only God , but we cannot accept Thy self-evaluation of 'omniscient'.

♦ Thy research output shows many lean years. Thy one major publication has sold well, especially when Thou opted for co-publishing with Gideon. But manifold are the authors thereof and other physics departments have not been able to replicate the results of some of Thy experiments, such as turning water into wine and parting the Red Sea.

♦ The creation of the Earth itself certainly counts as a major invention but developments in the theory of evolution cast doubt on whether it falls within the time period of this assessment.

Teaching

- Progress rates are very disappointing both between Christening and First Communion and from First Communion to the Great Big Final Assessment in the Sky. We are pleased to see that things should improve under the new Higher Education Statistical Agency when, rather than dividing the sheep from the goats Thou will also have extra categories such as 'Sheepish' and 'Goat with just a hint of sheep'. However, the cloning of extra sheep to boost Thy success rates is well out of order.

- Thy curriculum is rather dated and so we recommend you develop more entrepreneurial courses such as Creative Flock Management, The Effective Believer, and Messiah Studies.

- The teaching materials themselves contain too much smiting and begetting , especially before the deluge.

- Avoid using parables that do not have clearly defined learning outcomes.

- Face-to-face small group teaching in cold draughty old buildings should be phased out and we support Thy move into distance education by using epistles.

- Thy brochure claims that Thy graduates go on to higher level study in a land of milk and honey, but there is no hard evidence. Our own questionnaire surveys have had only limited success because those returned by drop-outs have been unreadable due to heavy scorching.

- We consider that Thy senior management team of twelve disciples is excessive. We recommend that you down-size to four, each of whom will have a clearly delineated portfolio of responsibilities for areas such as evangelism, overturning money-lenders' tables, denying thrice, etc.

The New Technologies

◆ Your use of IT is very limited and in future all Commandments should be set up as Web pages rather than delivered on tablets of stone.

◆ Thy Keynote Address on the Mount attracted many thousand customers but only those in the first three rows could actually hear anything.

◆ Your people have partaken of the forbidden Apple Macintosh and manifold are their platforms. From this day forward they shall cleave only unto PCs and they shall not covet their neighbours' Power Mac.

Equal Opportunities

◆ The appointment of Thy son smacks of nepotism and Fair Selection Procedures also do not appear to have been in place when he set up his management team.

◆ There would appear to be very few people with disabilities on Thy staff. We do not accept Thy argument that it is because Thy Son keeps healing them as speedily as Thou employ them.

◆ Thy data on ethnic origin is very poor. It is not sufficient to put all people in the same category, namely, 'In My own image'.

◆ Apart from one token mother figure, women appear to be relegated to foot-washing and general catering.

𝕱𝖎𝖓𝖆𝖓𝖈𝖊

- We commend thee for having fed Thy flock of students with seven Wonderloaves and a catering pack of fish fingers. Let Thy efficiency savings continue to bear fruit, for henceforth Thou shall only be awarded six loaves.

Here endeth our Report

And so God looked again on what He had created and saw that it was not 'very good'. Yea, verily, it was only 2.7 on a five point scale wherein 1 is the despis-ed number known as 'Very bad' and 5 rejoiceth in the name of 'Very good'.

'Good Heavens' He thundered 'It must be time for a little re-creation'.

This ancient text, which was discovered by a PhD student researching the history of quality assurance in Higher Education, suggests that Total Quality Management actually existed several thousand years earlier than scientists previously thought. (Apparently the document was meant to be ten and a half chapters long but the papyrus budget was cut by 25 per cent that year).

Soundings is grateful to Alan Woodley for the discovery of this document.

A winter's journey

Notes on the social democratic sublime

Ken Worpole

The secret heart of Stockholm is Slussen, which takes its name from the lock-gate or sluice where the inner waters of Stockholm's - and central Sweden's - lake and canal system pour into the open waters of the Baltic, just a few feet below the pavements of the old town, right in the heart of the city. Walking back to the hotel from the Kryp In, a small restaurant and jazz club in Gamla Stan, the old town, the temperature 5 degrees below zero, the snow frozen thick and still coming down, we take a short diversion, gingerly climbing down the icy steps, dropping below the streets, just to watch the black waters rush through the narrow, dark and brutal canal. It's the Stockholm of lost souls in Graham Greene's *England Made Me*. Freezing black waters, flecked with snow, rushing headlong into the Baltic as if escaping from some dark interior.

Yet even on a bitter morning, it is easy to forget the cold in the bustle of central Stockholm, the 'Venice of the North'. The giant Baltic ferries sail right into the heart of the city, just below the brown and yellow ochre cliffs of seventeenth and eighteenth-century buildings rising up from out of the water on the islands of Gamla Stan and Södermalm. Everybody ignores the ice and snow underfoot, and gets on with daily life as in any other city. But just a few stops from T Centralen, the central underground station, you step out into an extraordinary landscape that combines the aspirations of twentieth century Nordic architectural modernism, with a carefully constructed attempt to evoke the pagan burial mounds and desolate forests of pre-historic Sweden. This is the Stockholm Woodland Cemetery.

'*Pas de cimitière, pas de cité,*' shouted the Parisian crowds, when demonstrating against Haussman's plan to remove the cemeteries from central Paris in the 1870s. Cemeteries provide a gazetteer of a city's people, their beliefs, their family relationships and their trades. Stockholm's great twentieth-century cemetery, designed by Erik Gunnar Asplund and Sigurd Leweretz, was started in 1915 and not finally completed until 1961. It is one of the very few attempts in twentieth-century Europe to create a thoroughly new kind of urban cemetery. In doing so Asplund and Leweretz broke completely with both European and Islamic traditions - the city of the dead or paradise garden - and created a landscape in which the individual memorial was wholly subsumed within a more powerful landscape or 'natural' terrain.

Apart from the return to pre-historic forms, the influences were also rather painterly. As you enter the main gate, all you see is a view of a gentle but massive snow-covered grass knoll and an uninterrupted view of the iron-grey sky. One third/two-thirds: the classical landscape proportions, connected only by a vast granite cross that locks earth and sky together. The symbolic meaning of the cross remains in dispute. It is based on a recurring image in the work of Caspar David Friedrich, generally assumed to be German but in fact a Swedish national by birth, and rightly a pivotal figure in Simon Schama's recent epic, *Landscape and Memory*. In many of Friedrich's landscapes there is at least one wayfarer's cross, a sign of hope in an otherwise abandoned world. Asplund and Leweretz claimed that the cross was open to non-Christian interpretations, and quoted Friedrich himself: 'to those who see it as such, a consolation, to those who do not, simply a cross.' To the side of the cross is a path which leads up the hill to the Monumental Hall, a vast, angular, open plan colonnaded temple in a style that mixes National Romanticism with a rather aggressive functionalism. The views everywhere are of artificial ponds, earth mounds, oak circles, elm groves and natural pine forest, and it is deep in the last that the insignificant memorials and grave markers are mostly hidden.

The development of the cemetery and crematorium coincided with the rising influence of Swedish social democracy, particularly strong in Stockholm itself. Cremation was thought to foster a greater sense of equality in burial practices, eschewing the excessive differences of the ornate marble mausoleum at one extreme, and the pauper's grave at the other. A socially conscious aesthetic - influenced by William Morris and the English 'Art and Crafts' movement and emphasising the unity of art and life (or in this case art and death) - promoted the idea that death and bereavement were part of a shared, enduring human condition rather than a matter for wholly private, and sometimes ostentatious, grief. There was also a strong tradition of large processional funerals, particularly for working-class people, with hundreds following the coffin with standards and trade union banners held aloft. Ironically, this public and collective tradition was finally broken as a result of the success of social democracy itself. Traditionally most funerals were held on Saturday or Sunday, when people were free from work, but with the accomplishment of paid leave to attend funerals for close family and friends, the public funeral was transformed almost immediately, and irreversibly, into a private affair. Politics has so often been a story of unintended consequences, more tragic than comic, which only those with a developed sense of irony should take seriously.

Just such a funeral was taking place as I walked through the Monumental Hall: the men and women in dark overcoats shuffling and coughing as they waited for the hearse to arrive, some surreptitiously smoking from cigarettes held hidden behind their backs; a punk teenage girl with pink hair and spangled tights being glowered at by older family members. I took the train back into central Stockholm later with some of them. The electronic signs on the factory and office buildings we passed displayed the date, time and temperature: it was nine degrees below zero. I had gone to pay homage to a unique experiment in urban design and culture: an attempt to combine a modernist aesthetic with the spirit of collectivist social democracy and a respect for the enduring natural terrain, with all three ideals now frozen solid beneath the snow, and the temperature getting colder.

The next evening I flew to Örnsköldsvik, far in the north of Sweden on the Baltic coast, just a hundred or so miles from the Arctic circle. I and two colleagues had been invited over by the Swedish Cultural Ministry to exchange views about the future of public libraries, and each of us had been flown to a different part of the country to look at libraries and talk with staff and local politicians. Örnsköldsvik airport is about 30 kilometres inland from the town, and is located in a clearing in a forest. The plane landed, or so it seemed, in an empty snowfield, the lights of the aircraft cutting a bright swathe through the surrounding blizzard. But the most heart-numbing part of the trip was yet to come. Seven people boarded the airport bus, operated by a smiling middle-aged woman, who welcomed everybody on board, sold the tickets, shut the doors and roared off. Then, it seemed, we simply tobogganed down the mountain. The bus swayed, rocked, and glided down hills, over bridges, and round bends at a ferocious speed. There was no visible road to follow, just striped poles on both sides marking where the road should be, even though it had lain buried for months beneath packed ice. In the headlights, we rocketed through forests and hurtled along beneath the black sky, like Gorky's mad troika ride through Russia in *Dead Souls*. I could hardly breathe. Occasionally a car or timber truck came towards us, its headlights basking in the bright snow, blackening out the whole sky, but our driver didn't let up at all, keeping her foot pressed down on the accelerator and roaring through the narrow gaps.

It was Advent, and every so often we passed a a clapboard house in a clearing, silhouetted against the dark, and in each of the many windows were hundreds of lights and artificial candles, glowing and flickering. Each house was latticed with lights, every hallway, room and attic. The furniture, the dinner tables, the kitchens, the bedrooms with the children's toys were all stage-lit, with lights strung from the roof too, and even festooning some of the surrounding trees. The whole impression was of a series of fairy castles, of mythical gingerbread houses ablaze in the wood.

When the bus arrived in Örnsköldsvik - a small Baltic port handling largely timber and industrial machinery, and mostly shipping out to Russia, Estonia, Latvia and other late communist Baltic countries - I was dropped off at the hotel, opposite the harbour which was completely frozen over and covered with snow like a vast ice rink. The air was almost too cold to breathe, except through pursed lips. My ears stung. In the hotel room, a large modern room with kitsch paintings of tundra and forests, I poured a large whisky and carried on reading *The Poetics of Space*.

In this book, Gaston Bachelard attempts to create a phenomenology of the house, the room, the empty wardrobe, the drawer and even the small chest or box, as a way of understanding how and why humans relate to certain kinds of intimate space, and are in fact emotionally constructed by these associations and residual memories. By happy coincidence I came quite quickly to a chapter on the psychological associations and meanings of *lighted windows*. The lamp you see, also sees you. The light in the window is a form of a vigil, and through it, the house becomes human, keeping watch on us as we draw comfort from its illuminated presence. More poetically, Bachelard concludes that what we find almost magical about a cluster of lit houses at night is that, 'In such images we have the impression that the stars in heaven come to live on earth, that the houses of men form earthly constellations.' A good work of theory, such as this, is hard to find.

Arne was the architect of the Örnsköldsvik's new town library, and this is what I had travelled to see. It is already famous throughout Sweden, and beyond. The fact that Arne was a local architect, who had never designed a public library before, yet who had created such an accomplished and fully realised building, was in itself remarkable. On a previous visit I had been shown round the library several times by different people, but the following morning I was shown round by Arne himself.

The new Örnsköldsvik public library occupies one-third of a large modernist-vernacular building, triangular in plan, facing the harbour. The other two-thirds are taken up by the new town business centre and the local technical high school. All three are linked by an indoor street, a lively and bustling public space, with a cafe, an employment centre, an information bureau flanking the central aisle, along with the two main library entrances. As you first enter 'The Ark', as the building is called, you find yourself facing a large circular atrium, a rotunda, with book-lined galleries at first floor level. This great library dome covers the public street, and a bridge which crosses the circular basement performance area, leading beyond the library towards the business centre. In this open basement arena, a local choir may be rehearsing, a school group exhibiting paintings, or a local pianist practising Debussy, all to the benefit of the people passing overhead. The library shelves are open to view from the 'street', but are not directly accessible because they are on the first floor. The main entrances to the library, at ground floor level, lead into the adult fiction library on the left, the children's library on the right, through which you can walk upstairs or take a lift, and find yourself back in the public area again looking down on to the crowds below.

Arne tells me, with just a hint of bravura, that the rotunda is almost exactly the same diameter as that of the Stockholm City Library, one of the great library buildings of Europe, designed in the 1920s by Erik Gunnar Asplund - the very same person responsible for the Woodland Cemetery - which has provided a reference point for much international library architecture since then. It testifies to the self-confident politics of this small town that they commissioned a new public library of such impressive grandeur and size. For Örnsköldsvik is a town of just 20,000 people, with a further 40,000 to be found in the surrounding hinterland, made up mostly of suburbs or hamlets attached to paper plants and timber processing factories. There are also many small farms within the district boundaries.

The new library, I am told, probably represents a final great civic bequest by a local government tradition which, as in many other parts of Europe, is never likely to have the same confident spending power again. Throughout Europe there has been an absolute transfer of spending from the public sector to the market-place - education, transport, health, pensions, even policing - and public taxation is no longer seen by most people as the necessary, if restrictive, good that it once was. In Britain even taxation itself has been partially privatised through the new National Lottery, a 'voluntary' levy to pay for what were traditionally public goods such as village halls, opera houses and national archives. Yet the new Örnsköldsvik library wins universal approval throughout the district, and is already the centre of local life.

Most of Arne's previous commissions have been designs for housing, offices and small factories. He had never been interested particularly in libraries as buildings, but now he was fascinated by the richness of the architectural and social tradition, and he told me that it had been the most important project he had ever undertaken. When his firm had been awarded the job, he had started by visiting libraries elsewhere in Sweden, in Finland and Germany. Asplund's Stockholm library remained the most influential reference point, although that had been designed as a civic temple to knowledge, whereas the Örnsköldsvik library had been intended as the town's 'living room' or 'salon'. This sea-change in the perception of the public library, not simply as a repository of information and knowledge, but as a meeting place of an educated and informed democracy, is one of the great paradigm shifts in civic architecture in this century.

Asplund's Stockholm library represents the most formal expression of the 'temple of knowledge' tradition, with its almost sarcophagus-like front elevation, the wide steps, the imposing front door and the rising bulk of the rotunda appearing to suggest a forbidden inner chamber. Inside, it is even more severe. The lobby is an ante-chamber of dark marble decorated by a frieze exhibiting stories from the *Iliad*, by the artist Ivar Johnsson, and the atmosphere is oppressive and gloomy. Once inside, there stands another marble portal, a dark, narrow staircase climbing up into the central rotunda itself, and symbolically leading from the darkness of the entrance hall into the light of the great library room. The library is a highly formal arrangement of inner and outer chambers, decorated in art deco style, and represents a last flowering of Nordic Classicism, before the final and happy arrival of Scandinavian social democracy and architectural modernism, the era of timber (particularly light softwoods), stainless steel, airiness, light and glass. Inside the rotunda, there is a cantilevered book gallery running the circumference of the great room, which when I was last there one bitterly cold autumn evening was gloomy and lit by a melancholy yellow light from within.

A number of different architectural models now compete to embody the ideals of the public library - and of public, accessible knowledge - in the modern city. Three paradigms dominate: the library as a temple of knowledge; the library as an enclosed arcade or town square; or the library as cultural department store. Until the 1970s Asplund's Stockholm library prevailed as the dominant model of the traditional 'gallery library', which deliberately provided only space enough to browse between the stacks, with little space for social or convivial uses. In the 1980s, in Sweden and Britain, libraries were increasingly modelled on department stores, presenting books, records, videos face forward, occupying large open plan, single storey buildings, with windows on to the street to display the 'goods' inside. This is probably still the dominant model in Britain, with the new - and enormously popular - Croydon central library out-doing Marks & Spencer for escalators, integrated interior design, opening hours, and crowds. In Sweden, though, the department store model is no longer in favour, and a renewed concern for public and civic values has led to the design of libraries, such as the one in Örnsköldsvik, based on re-creating the town square or street indoors, with civic services such as the library, the information department, education advice services, congregated around an inner street, with a cafe and even shops. Within the library space, armchairs are grouped together to create a living room effect, where elderly people and students often sit for hours reading the newspapers, gossiping. In the winter months, when temperatures regularly fall to minus 20 degrees, Örnsköldsvik library comes into its own as the town salon.

'Three paradigms dominate: the library as a temple of knowledge, as an enclosed arcade or town square, or as cultural department store'

The building has been a stunning success, and I got the feeling that the challenge, now completed, has left Arne restless. Over several days, I was in and out of the library more than a dozen times, and always the inner street was packed with people, meeting, gossiping, promenading. On my last morning with the library staff, I was told we were all to have coffee and cakes before the library opened, a small celebration to mark the end of a successful school holiday programme. At 9.30 we all gathered in the staff area to light candles and sing folk songs. There were 25 full and part-time staff running the library - all women. And that day, in addition, there was me. We danced in a circle, singing, did a 'strip the willow' processional, holding hands, all through the library, up and down spiral staircases, in and out of all the offices, through the public foyer, and back to the staff area, singing. One final circle dance, and a long song about all the different animals, with gestures - we waggled our bums like rabbits, woofed woofed like dogs, miaowed like cats, flapped our arms like birds - and then sat down exhausted for cakes and coffee. Then we talked about book acquisition policies, current levels of stock-holding, the demographic make-up of the library users, and so on. My Swedish hosts effected the transition from carnivalesque to professional decorum with barely a flicker of self-consciousness in their traditional reserve.

Arne picked me up at the Stadshotell at three in the afternoon; we had arranged to have tea. I was due to return to Stockholm early the next morning. However, he was keen to drive me into the hills above Örnsköldsvik, from where we would be able to get a bird's-eye view of the town, the port and the bay. We drove out along the harbour road, past the endless stacks of oozing, resinous Russian birch logs stacked on the quays like pyres, past the Gothic, castellated, wooden railway station (now permanently closed), past the ship repair yard, past the oil terminal, and followed the road round into the next bay. Then we took a sharp right, and climbed steeply into the hills until we came to the top. Here the snow was still thick and iron-hard. There was a weather station with a look-out platform.

Behind us, to the west, there was an endless succession of snow-bound hills, with frozen lakes iced in between the folds. Each lake had a dull, gun-metal sheen. The air was almost blue and slightly opaque, draining the scenery of colour, rather like yet another painting by Caspar David Friedrich, one of his elemental, melancholy winter landscapes, abandoned by God. To the east, beyond Örnsköldsvik and the lattice-work of rivers and lakes linking it up to the sea, the sun made everything glow. The small suburb surrounding the paper mill on the far side of the bay stood washed in the late afternoon sunlight, and glowed golden too. Arne says he never tires of this view. He pointed in the direction where his own island summer house is to be found, where he goes most weekends - except in the deepest winter - to sail, to fish and to sleep.

We drove back to town, and went for a drink in the new English pub on the quay. I asked him if the water was clean these days, what with the paper mills strung out along the shore-line, wafting out steam or smoke from the great industrial chimneys. He tells me that recent legislation has greatly improved things, and that people now swim in the harbour as they used to do when he first came to the town.

'Isn't it too cold, even in the summer?'

'No, not at all. Some people swim all the year round, even when there is ice.'

I feigned disbelief.

'Sure, particularly after a sauna. You get accustomed to it. I grew up on an island outside Stockholm. Every Friday night we had a sauna, and we made a hole in the ice outside, and we jumped in when we got very hot. After you have been in the water you can walk round in the snow, completely naked, for five to ten minutes and still feel warm. Even in the middle of winter, say minus ten degrees.'

Arne went on to tell me more about his childhood.

'Because we lived on an island, our parents had to teach us how to survive in the ice and the snow. We had to learn what to do if we fell through the ice, which happened to me several times in my childhood. You see, in the winter we had to walk to school across the ice because the boat could not be used, and the school was on another island.'

So how *do* you survive I asked? This had been a great terror instilled into me during my childhood: the unspeakable horrors and awful death suffered by those who ventured onto thin ice and fell through, their bodies only recovered after the thaw, and of the other children who had gone to their rescue and in turn had also drowned. My mother told stories of such incidents as a warning, painting a grim picture - which years later I finally saw realised in Eisenstein's *Alexander Nevsky* - of a never-ending succession of capsizes, attempted rescues, and further drownings, bodies filling the water like logs.

'There is one simple rule: as soon as you fall in, you must turn to face the way you were coming from, and then climb out - as quickly as possible. Logically the ice you were walking on must be stronger than the ice you were walking towards. But we always carried two small steel pins, on a string around our necks, which were used to grip the ice to pull yourself out. But you have to be quick! Once your clothes become heavy with water, and your muscles start to get - do you say 'cramp'

- then you are finished. Lost.'

We sat for several hours, talking, occasionally looking out beyond the harbour, watching the late evening sun retreating west, the night sky clouding over with inky whorls and pink tendrils, casting longer and darker shadows over the whole bay. Arne tried to explain a Swedish folk saying, but it remained untranslatable. 'We have the same expression to mean to sit waiting for the dawn and also to fool somebody.' But I never worked out what it was, or how these two very different things could share a common metaphor. We ate baked perch, with potatoes and salad; outside the occasional car or timber truck swished by on winter tyres, studded with metal pins, crunching the salted roads. Örnsköldsvik seemed such a remote and simple idyll. It was easy to understand how people earned a living and fulfilled their lives - they cut down trees, they worked in paper factories, they fished or farmed, they built their own houses, went to the library, joined trade unions and political parties, went to church, had children, perhaps had affairs, and one day died.

Yet, even this fairly remote town in Northern Sweden now had a small immigrant community, made up of several hundred Bosnian refugees who, on the several occasions I visited it, were nowhere to be seen. I imagined they had been settled in a couple of the large public housing blocks on the edge of town and largely left to fend for themselves on welfare. How they might ever adjust to this austere, Protestant setting, I can't imagine - or whether they would ever be made fully welcome. But this is one of the key *leit-motifs* of the European economic and social future: that even the smallest of towns or cities will not remain untouched by the great exoduses and diasporas of global migration, and even fair-haired, neutralist and somewhat isolationist Sweden - though often a generous host in the past to refugees - is now becoming as multi-cultural as France, Germany or Britain.

When it finally grew too dark to make out the harbour jetty, we paid the bill and we left. Arne escorted me back to the hotel; we shook hands and wished each other goodnight - and goodbye. The following morning I was on the plane looking down on Örnsköldsvik disappearing fast behind me, its hinterland of lakes and forests frozen a bluish white, its harbour a cracked jigsaw puzzle of ice, as I flew back south to Stockholm in the cloudless, golden light.

Presumed innocence
Christine Alhadeff

Blake Morrison, *As If*, Granta, £14.99, 255pp
Gitta Sereny, *The Case of Mary Bell*, new edition, Pimlico, £10, 333pp
Lorrie Moore (ed), *The Faber Book of Contemporary Stories about Childhood*, Faber, £15.99, 415pp

In February 1993, in Liverpool, two ten-year-old boys abducted a two-year-old called James Bulger from a shopping centre, walked with him for two and a half miles to a railway line and there, as darkness fell, with bricks and an iron bar battered him to death. Some deaths are emblematic, tipping the scales, and little James's death - green fruit shaken from the bough, an ear of grain sown back in the earth - seemed like the murder of hope: the unthinkable thought of, the undoable done. If child-killings are the worst killings, then a *child* child-killing must be the worse than worst, a new superlative in horror. In that spring cold fear, it was as if there'd been a breach in nature. Those nameless boys had killed not just a child but the idea of childhood. Ten-year-olds were looked at with a new suspicion, and toddlers kept on tight reins.

And so Blake Morrison plunges us into the world of *As If*, at once compelling and compassionate, irritating and confusing. His aim was to reverse John Major's injunction that 'we must condemn a little more and understand a little less', but, in presenting us so nakedly with the contradictions and moral confusion of the current social climate, the understanding Morrison hopes to achieve ultimately remains elusive.

In her book *The Case of Mary Bell*, published in a new edition in the wake of the Bulger trial, Gitta Sereny shows that the infamous Mary Bell, who murdered two boys in Newcastle in 1965, was mostly viewed by the general public as a 'one off', a gross deviation from the norm, and not representative of the general condition. In contrast, the sentencing of Jon Venables and Robert Thompson was felt to carry the full force of society's current anxiety about its structures; a fear, among fears, that childhood is under threat; that children are more than they were, no longer the happy innocents and idealists that Morrison evokes by his references to Henry Treece's 1958 novel *The Children's Crusade*.

Morrison is concerned to explore this anxiety alongside the specific events of James Bulger's death and the subsequent trial. For these events were felt to be of mythic significance; the video images of toddler James being led away with his hand apparently trustingly given to Jon Venables were seen as iconographic, deeply resonating with our notions of childhood and our desire to preserve it as a place of innocence and trust.

In fact, childhood is a relatively modern invention. Once examined, it reveals itself as telling us less about the inherent nature of children's experience than it does about the needs and attitudes of the society by which it was constructed. Philippe Ariès' book *Centuries of Childhood (1962)* charts a gradual development: unknown before the twelfth century, childhood gradually took shape in the seventeenth century to emerge as something that we might recognise by the nineteenth. Central to this evolution was the idea of innocence, an idea pivotal to the legal system which Morrison attacks. Jon Venables and Robert Thompson were tried as adults - deemed capable of moral judgement and responsibility. And yet, as they were found guilty of 'unparalleled evil and barbarity', the boys were judged not in comparison with the adults who have committed similar crimes, but in comparison with the assumed innocence of all other children - the innocence which, once forfeited, allowed Venables and Thompson to be vilified as monsters, outside the pale of society's definitions.

In fact, as Gitta Sereny tells us, child murders by other children remain rare - on average, once a decade. But, in her new appendix about the Bulger case, she predicts that such crimes will become more frequent. The basis for her view is the concern she shares with Morrison about the impact on children of their experiences at the hands of 'increasingly troubled adults' in a society in which no group is willing or able to exercise authority and where lives are ruled by economics rather than 'thought or morality'.

Both Morrison and Sereny expose the more fundamentally 'criminal' guilt of the courts for their failure to allow evidence about the family backgrounds of Mary Bell, Venables and Thompson, who had, each in their turn, suffered disturbance, rejection and violence. Witnesses such as Eileen Vizard, a consultant child psychiatrist, who made an assessment of Jon Venables, were only allowed to comment on whether the boys would have known the difference between 'right' and 'wrong'. The question 'why' was never asked: the trial was limited to 'where and when, who and how.'

However, it is in Morrison's explanation of these legally inadmissible biographical details, that my sense began to deepen of 'something not quite right'; something that confuses where it is meant to clarify. For, in his insistence that we should recognise these children as damaged, Morrison clings to a version of childhood innocence - their guilt is simply displaced, onto the parents, the court, the school, the videos, the adults who failed to intervene, the society who failed to understand.

From the opening pages of *As If* there is something about Morrison's writing that both engages and disturbs. The lack of belief in a moral consensus leads understandably but uncomfortably to his use of his own experience as the only base line for judgement; the 'me too' frame work which is intended to promote empathy and insight, tends at times to reveal rather too much about Morrison and about his family, at the expense of his subject matter. The lack of boundaries, the feeling of something inappropriate, begins to intrude.

Morrison claims a license to speculate on what James felt, what his mother felt, what Venables and Thompson felt; ultimately deciding that things merely got out of hand; that the children were tired and afraid of punishment if they returned with the stolen child. There is no evidence for this. In fact, what Morrison describes is that, like most of us, including the people who came to throw stones and abuse the boys outside the court room, he was both drawn towards and repelled by the events. There was something Morrison could not face in the nature of these children's experience. This was their *intention* to hurt and damage, even kill. And their expression of murderous and destructive fantasises was the reflection of the destruction and damage of which they felt themselves to be victims. Most children retain the capacity to preserve the line between fantasy and such acting out in reality. Why Thompson and Venables were unable to do so may be the thing most helpful to understand. But first we have to face up to their actions.

On the page, Morrison's writing often seems beautiful but overblown; its Shakespearean echoes remind us of the scale of the tragedy but also feel indulgent, and distracting from the grubby awfulness of the events. Reading his work aloud,

Morrison adopts a tone that paradoxically flattens and normalises the content with a confusing reasonableness. He seems to want to reassure both himself and his public that there is nothing out of the ordinary here; we all know about these things - at the same time as telling us we are in the presence of the unthinkable.

Despite these contradictions I feel moved and involved. Morrison apologises: 'I feel ashamed of my fantasies. They're inappropriate, I know. I'm a bundle of inappropriateness, a night-wandering man pierced with the remembrance of a grievous wrong.' He tell us of Venables' unbearable sobbing; his screaming tantrums when pressed to discuss what had actually occurred. The jurors felt discomfited, even traumatised, in having to disregard such distress. And yet, is it not possible that Venables was expressing not just childish upset, but the anguish of being caught in a dilemma which is terrible whether one is a child or an adult: that of knowing what one has done to be awful but being unable to face it. Linking these actions to his family history and environment would of course be essential, as Morrison explains. But without also truly addressing the awfulness of what has been done it is difficult to imagine how either of these boys could really be helped towards a new life.

In seeking to redress the harsh moral judgement of the legal system, Morrison shifts so much of the responsibility for what occurred on to others that we are left feeling - once again - that such acts have no place in our notion of childhood. Morrison merely flips the moral coin; all blame becomes no blame. He confuses compassion with an invitation to avoid any uncomfortable recognition of the darker horrors of the psyche and, in the process, deprives us of the chance of real understanding.

Adults write about children with a curious amalgam of perspective. Blake Morrison believes that it is impossible to remember what he really felt at ten years old. So it is, in *The Faber Book of Contemporary Stories about Children*. These are adult versions of childhood, less concerned to explore the experience of children in relation to other children, than with children confronted with the contradictions and hypocrisies of the adults on whom they depend. In this sense the book is more about the collision of childhood with adulthood than about childhood itself.

Despite their predominantly disillusioned tone these stories seem to reflect how much we remain preoccupied with childhood - our need to redress its wrongs, our hankering after its capacity for truth. Sometimes with painful reluctance, sometimes with anger or delight, the children in this book confront their experience.

Gryphon, by Charles Baxter, describes a crazy but entertaining substitute teacher who dispenses, with normal lessons in favour of her own more bizarre preoccupations. Inevitably, she goes too far and is removed. Life returns to normal but the pleasures of her brief regime are savoured as part of the essential secrecy of childhood.

More serious is the wonderful story by Edna O'Brien called 'My Mother's Mother', in which she explores her excruciating ambivalence towards her mother, and finally recognises the equal pleasures of presence and absence, the uncomfortable balance of loving and hating.

The range of these stories is enormous. Though they may tell us more about the adult world than that of childhood, they provide a rich resource of interest and pleasure through which to explore this very contemporary confusion.

Questions for Government
Kevin Davey

Will Hutton, *The State to Come*, Vintage, £4.99
Geoff Mulgan, *Connexity: How to Live in a Connected World*, Chatto & Windus, £17.99

New Labour has an identity problem. It is far clearer about what it is not than about what it is. It knows more about what it won't than about what it will do. The hardest issues have been dubbed questions for government, not for opposition. This absence of detail has meant that interested parties, special pleaders, seers, lobbyists, opponents and the uninhibited have faced a choice: to cross their fingers and hope that all will be well, or to rush in where Labour apparently fears to tread.

Believing it irresponsible to remain mute at this turning point in British politics, *Observer* editor Will Hutton and Demos director Geoff Mulgan have each picked their favourite moment from a long and swirling series of attempts to redefine the party's purpose, in order to build something more strategic and ambitious upon it.

Only eighteen months ago, stakeholding was Labour's big idea. Companies had other responsibilities than their shareholders, services had a plurality of accountabilities. The party quietly disposed of this particular rhetoric when the trade unions, these days living on borrowed institutional time, welcomed it as an inclusive and meaningful language for politics. Will Hutton, like many others on the left, is unwilling to dispose of this idea so readily and in *The State to Come* he beefs up the case he made for stakeholding in *The State We're In*.

And stakeholding is not the only song no longer on the party's playlist. These days we don't hear too much of communitarianism, the American counter-liberal rhetoric imported into British political discourse by Demos. But in *Connexity* Geoff Mulgan deepens the communitarian argument for a review of liberal categories like freedom, the individual and independence, insisting that our biggest problems should be seen as 'disorders of freedom'.

Both books are accessible and informed polemics on complex and challenging issues. If they are any indication of the quality of the public debate that will follow the election, the audience for political economy and political philosophy is set to grow. Taken together, they also suggest the outline of a new and radical consensus on democratisation, the role of government and forms of economic regeneration that are much less deferential to longstanding interests than the Blair project.

Hutton blows the whistle on Britain's timid investor class, finding it guilty of abandoning its responsibility for 'high risk innovation at the forefront of technology' in favour of a short term lust for real estate and trading profits. Flexible and social democratic in outlook, Hutton insists that 'the fulcrum around which the good society turns is an equitable distribution of work and income'. He therefore directs most of his critique towards the central categories of Conservative thought: the failing chimeras of the free market and individual choice, the demonisation of taxation and government for a common good, and the irresponsible equation of efficiency with the minimisation of costs. With an articulate anger he checklists the many painful shortcomings of a culture in which 'Contract is King' and trust and the long term are marginal.

Given that the domestic economic policies of the major parties have all but converged, Hutton is swinging a double edged sword. The convictions he opposes have actually made their way unchecked, albeit a little scarred and discredited, into the very frontline of Labour's thinking. Hutton acknowledges that Anglo-American neo-liberal thought has had a major impact on the centre left and, laying short term considerations to one side, rises to the occasion. He urges 'extreme scepticism' about the 'major surgery' any Labour attempt to greatly reduce the proportion of GDP reinvested as public expenditure would require. He warns that 'unless an ascendant body of ideas can be assembled, underpinned by a political philosophy that incorporates a different world view and policy direction, Labour will find in office that it governs in essence as a nicer group of Conservatives'. Of course, one might take the view that the political *raison d'être* of a party is a question for opposition - where it must pass the test of public support - before it becomes a question of government. But better late than never.

Having registered his doubts, Hutton returns to the task of updating and refurbishing our notions of the public good, progressive taxation, trade unionism, social insurance, and public spending - few of which have seen active service for the last twenty years. All appear to be in good working order, if a little changed in appearance.

While most of Hutton's policy recommendations coincide with Labour's stated intentions, he places greater emphasis on the need to reform the Treasury, and to change the rules governing the work of investment fund managers. He stresses how important it is to tax pension fund dividends - the best way to discourage these large institutional investors from wreaking industrial havoc in pursuit of high returns - and the need for institutionalised investor research.

Hutton dismisses the much voiced objection that stakeholding represents a return to corporatism or the importation of a German economic model. His vision has much more in common with that of Blair's inner circle: 'a more inclusive, fairer, higher investing Britain with a well functioning democracy'. The real difference is that he addresses the concerns of a wider range of members of Labour's diverse coalition of supporters. As a result, his vision of stakeholding resonates with something of the coherence necessary to integrate most of Labour's tactical and temporary coalition into a long term and radical project in goverment. But there is a price to pay. Hutton has had to name as enemies some of those that Labour now considers its friends: the City of London, and defenders of our unwritten constitution. You can't please all of the people all of the time, and at some point New Labour will have to stop trying.

Geoff Mulgan also believes that traditional conceptions of liberalism and socialism have become unworkable. But he thinks that this is because they draw on notions of freedom - as escape, or liberation from constraint - that are unworkable in our increasingly interdependent society. His book is a lengthy exposition of a fairly simple idea: that however we feel, we do not live in isolation from others, insulated from the effects of our actions. Ours is a new age of 'connexity', and governments and citizens have a responsibility to create and foster institutions and personalities that are appropriate in this new social environment.

Like Hutton, Mulgan believes that the state is benevolent and retains many of its capacities, even in an era of economic globalisation, but that it is possible to have too much of a good thing. Governments should 'provide a framework of predictability, but leave more space for self organisation'. He favours leaner, more intelligent forms of government than those we have known: states that welcome the pooling of sovereignties, that form reciprocating partnerships for themselves and for others, governments that work by reshaping cultures rather than by imposing legislation.

I doubt that Geoff Mulgan enjoyed the election campaign that followed the publication of his book. I imagine him following its pantomime routines and demands for applause with some impatience and distaste. 'Inherited forms, made up of elections, political parties, manifestoes, opinion polls, public meeetings, have become stuck', he argues. They are 'at odds with the culture of connexity that favours interactivity, reciprocity, openness'. Instead, Mulgan offers a vista of reformed and decentralised government complemented by deliberative forums, citizens' juries, and assemblies drawn by lot.

Something of a theoretical magpie, Mulgan assembles concepts and examples that support his case: evolutionary psychology, games theory, communitarianism, systems theory. What glitters in each is the concept of reciprocity, Mulgan's new Universal Political Principle, essential for the management of all relationships from private household arrangements to international summits.

These are not books for the faint hearted. Hutton risks unpopularity - and possibly blame, as Labour's coalition begins to exfoliate - by identifying institutional enemies. Mulgan's critique is perhaps more unsettling, and even less likely to win friends, identifying conceptual enemies even closer to home. But it was about time someone scanned the horizon, giving us notice of the shocks and pleasures to come.

A lost youth
Elizabeth Julian

Rose Tremain, *The Way I Found Her*, Sinclair-Stevenson, £15.99, 359pp

There is a moment in 'The Way I Found Her' when Lewis Little, Tremain's 13 year-old protagonist, substitutes the image of Ingrid - 'the sixteen-year-old sister of my friend Carl at Beckett Bridges School' - for that of Valentina, the 'crazy, romantic, gigantic Russian' (aged 41) with whom he is 'in love'. When Ingrid vanishes Lewis is left waiting, 'holding out my arms, for Valentina to come back'.

This could have been a book about a boy who fancies his mother. He tells us, 'what I thought was that the most beautiful thing in the world would be to be born out of Valentina's vagina and be lifted up on to her stomach and given one of her huge breasts to suck'. This vision of infantile bliss is indicative of the conflict raging within Lewis Little, as he struggles to reconcile his precocious sensitivity to the adult relationships by which he is surrounded with the more childish aspects of his nature. Poised on the brink of adolescence, racked with ambivalence, Lewis struggles to contain the tide of emotions by which he is suddenly flooded. Perhaps his erotic fixation on Valentina Gavril, rich and famous author of medieval romances, is best understood as the consequence of this rather painful but very exciting passage out of childhood.

Unlike Tremaine's previous novel *Sacred Country* (1992), which depicted its transsexual hero/ine Mary/Martin as part of a community of displaced souls, *The Way I Found Her* has only one narrator. Like *Sacred Country*, and Tremain's earlier work, this latest (her seventh) is a profoundly psychological novel. There are other characters, but the narrative is very much Lewis's. And there are none of the historical trappings of *Restoration* (1989), or of many of the short stories. This novel is set in the present, and written from the point of view of one boy. It is a brave achievement, to have staked so much on one character - and one so young.

The action takes place in Paris, where Lewis's mother Alice is working on a translation of Valentina's latest novel, while Valentina herself tries to finish it. But the story starts a day earlier - 'I could describe it as the day before my real life began' - 'with the moment when I noticed that my mother had become a beautiful woman'. Alice's 'fantastic, gorgeous beauty' is a revelation to her son, a fact confirmed in the faces of strangers. For the reader, Alice's beauty is a salient characteristic. Its effect on Lewis is to distance him from her; or rather, this new and different apprehension of his mother signifies that they are moving apart. For this journey to Paris which they make together, leaving Lewis's father home alone, turns out, paradoxically, to be a separation: 'I made an imaginary diagram of our two minds, Alice's and mine, and they were like two planets or stars zooming further and further away from each other'.

When Lewis goes to France he leaves his childhood self-consciously behind. On the first page Alice is trying to mend Action Man Elroy. When she gives up, and Lewis kicks his broken toy under the bed, he imagines that lying in the darkness and dust with Elroy is 'the boy I was when I imagined Elroy was real'. In Paris, he tells us, he felt 'about eighteen'. But as precocious and grown-up as he is, there are moments when Lewis misses his closeness with his mother. And when Alice seems 'distracted and far away', it is to Elroy that Lewis's thoughts turn: 'If Elroy had been there, ready for action with his beret on, I would have said to him: "Your mission is to infiltrate Alice's heart."'

But by the time Lewis realises that Alice has been 'neglecting me', he has latched on to Valentina's very different beauty: 'there was something really beautiful about her, something as beautiful and soft as snow. I wanted to walk into this snow ...' As his mother becomes increasingly self-absorbed and remote, Lewis concentrates his needs around the glamorous and exotic Valentina. Her emotional and demonstrative personality appeals to him, and could not be more different from Alice. There is something deliciously trashy about Valentina, author of bestsellers, with her cigarettes, her perfume and lipstick. She hardly speaks to Lewis without calling him 'darling'. Even her dog Sergei makes him feel like Arthur Miller, walking along in Marilyn's shadow.

From the moment when Valentina is lost, this novel becomes the narrative of Lewis's quest to find her. He describes the fateful moment, the last time he saw her, with nostalgiac longing, 'Certain moments in a life are in another tense: they are *going to become*. And only when you get to that other tense do they reveal to you what they were and what they meant ... and you think, if only I had understood what was going to happen and prevented it...'

But what is it that has he lost? This 13 year-old boy who loves the 'absolute total sadness' of Romeo and Juliet, a feeling he shares with Tremain's other protagonists. There is something terrible about their sorrow, a grief at the heart of her fiction. Lewis's mother, he tells us, is 'hardly ever happy anywhere, in any season'. In this novel it is the Russian characters - Valentina's mother and her friend Grigory Panin, and the memory of her father Anton - who bear the heaviest load. Of Mrs Gavrilovich Lewis observes: 'She had the blues. The blues were a thing Russians were born with. They lay in their prams, weeping for the greyness of the sky.' And yet who can resist such writing? For if Tremain's plots are tragic, their protagonists heartbroken, bereft, and profoundly altered, the pleasure of her texts is in their language; her simple, brilliant vocabulary; her terse, deadpan humour; and the wry observations of human social behaviour which she voices through her characters. On the Paris metro, for example, Lewis describes how 'A guy got on and started to play the guitar and sing to us. When he'd finished and was going round with the hat, he said: "If this experience has been disagreeable to you in any way, please inform me." But nobody informed him.' Or on the aeroplane, Tremaine hilariously captures Lewis's combination of adolescent nonchalance with childlike self-importance: '"What are you writing?" asked Alice. "Nothing much", I said. "Just a private theory."' It is sometimes hard to say why Tremain is so funny. What is certain is that her humour lightens the load which the reader of her fiction must bear.

Sacred Country's Mary/Martin was partly defined by her reading: *Black's Book of Magic*, and the *Dictionary of Inventions* help to establish her identity. Likewise in this novel Lewis's books are crucial markers of his, and the novel's trajectory. They are *Le Grand Meaulnes* - Alain-Fournier's classic which, Lewis learns, has been read by everyone with a French education - and Dostoevsky's *Crime and Punishment*.

Lewis decides to translate *Meaulnes*, a project with which Valentina becomes involved: 'When you begin a book and you already know in the first line that everything is in the past, this makes you worry so for the character... Because the thing he is writing about will turn out to be the most important thing in his life, you see?' Valentina's words resonate, for this novel too is narrated in the past tense, and at the moment of narration Lewis Little remains full of regret. The identification with his mother which Lewis's translation work involves - for translation is her work, too - simultaneously evokes the feelings of separation and exile which permeate both novels. Nostalgia is the theme of *Meaulnes* - its two protagonists, both adolescent boys - committed to searching and longing, for a lost girl and a lost youth.

Lewis's reading of *Crime and Punishment* serves as a backdrop to the plot of the novel's longer, second half - when Valentina's Russian past erupts in Lewis's present, and precipitates the novel's great crisis. As Lewis conducts his investigation, he identifies himself with Porphiry Petrovich, Dostoevsky's phlegmatic detective. But when Didier - the philosopher-roofer who Lewis is certain is his mother's lover - becomes identified with Rashkolnikov, it is clear that Lewis is tracking more than Valentina.

L ike *Sacred Country*, *The Way I Found Her* is haunted by images of flight which seem to represent Tremain's sense of our wilder ambitions, the fantastic dreams which too often end in tragedy. This poetic aspect of her writing, the metaphorical connections which crisscross the narrative, are more successful than the plot of this novel, whose latter stages are increasingly implausible and unnecessarily complicated. My impression was that Tremain had got sidetracked, caught up in tangled narrative threads. But the novel succeeds where Tremain has succeeded before, in conveying something of the tremendous difficulty of self-realisation; the pain intrinsic to human identity; the rites of passage which leave us changed, devastated, frozen. In excruciating detail she describes how alone we are, how desperately we crave, and the suffering that accompanies our passions. For comfort, we must look to the words themselves. And this is where Lewis himself must look, for he too is a writer.

The Millenial Malady?
James Souter

Elaine Showalter, *Hystories: hysteria and culture at the end of the century*, Picador, £16.99, 231pp

Across the centuries hysteria's ability to change and incorporate a seemingly limitless set of behaviours and symptoms means that very different and often contradictory disease formulations have prevailed. The term derives from *hystera*, the greek word for uterus. Classical records speak of strange symptoms in women - convulsive attacks, random pains, sensations of choking - produced by the womb wandering freely around the body. With advances in anatomy, and the centring of hysteria in the nervous system, hysteria became a disease of the mind, in which unconscious desires were converted into pathological changes and physical symptoms. Women, then seen as the nervous sex, were, as now, the majority of its sufferers - but the shift to 'nerves' opened up the possibility that men could also be hysterical. Now seen as a wholly psychological condition, hysteria suggests behaviour that produces the *appearance* of disease.

Hysteria, of course, has never been just a medical category. Knowledges of the condition - its theories, treatments and therapies - are produced within particular cultural contexts. If we consider hysteria less in terms of discrete psychopathology, and more as a mimetic disorder expressive of conflicts and anxieties within a culture, then a different history is possible. To talk of hysteria as a disease entity which has remained stable through time is to impose order on a medical category which has always been something of a 'taxonomic joker'. Showalter argues that terminologies may change, symptoms may decline or disappear, but there is always a 'quantity of hysterical energy' present. Hysteria is part of the psychopathology of everyday life and the 1990s, she argues, 'epidemic' hysterical times.

Showalter is a feminist literary critic and a historian of medicine, and she draws on both these disciplines. In *The Female Malady* (1985) she argued that hysteria was in some way the quintessential female malady'; a pejorative synonym for femininity; the book, despite now well-rehearsed critiques, firmly put hysteria on the feminist agenda. A particularly innovative feature of *The Female Malady* was its inclusion of a chapter on male hysteria in the First World War (a theme beautifully evoked by Pat Barker in *The Regeneration Trilogy*). Like nineteenth century middle-class women, the men were trapped in a closed and intolerable situation over which they had no control and, as a result experienced high levels of anxiety. With few psychological skills for expressing their anxiety directly, they 'adopted' *the primitive language of somatic symptom formation.*

Hystories marks the move from an interest in hysteria as individual and female to a more universal and cultural phenomenon. Her concern here is with hysterical epidemics as 'cultural narratives', for hysteria can take individual, mass or epidemic forms. Unlike outbreaks of mass hysteria which are usually spontaneous, short-lived and localised, epidemics of hysteria develop and spread over time. According to Showalter they require three basic conditions. They are the result of a complex interaction between physician-enthusiasts and theorists, unhappy vulnerable patients, and supportive cultural environments. This model allows her to link past epidemics, such as the mass outbreaks of 'female invalidism' in the late nineteenth century culminating with Charcot and Freud, with modern hysterical epidemics such as Anorexia and Bulimia, and the more recent psychogenic syndromes such as Gulf War Syndrome, Chronic Fatigue Syndrome (ME), Recovered Memory and Alien Abduction. These are potentially global phenomena but Showalter is particularly concerned with the United States, which she characterises as an hysterical 'hot zone'.

The amplification process goes through the following stages. A doctor must define, name and publicise the disorder and then attract patients into its community. The doctor must resolve the many confusing symptoms into a coherent theoretical explanation and advocate a systematic treatment or cure. These diagnosticians (the best of whom are charismatic) are linked to influential institutions (clinics, medical schools, etc) from where they advertise prototypes of patients. Self-help books broad enough to catch many variations personalise these disorders. The media disseminate information. Patients experience a bewildering range of symptoms but once they see their problems reflected in the prototype, they come to believe that the laws of a disorder describe their lives and seek the aid of a therapist, and embark on a 'career' which could well become a permanent way of life.

Epidemics of hysteria, Showalter argues, are not new to the contemporary period, and seem to peak at the ends of centuries: the Salem witch trials in the 1690s; the social crises of the 1890s. It is therefore unsurprising that, as we approach the end of the twentieth century, at a time when people are concerned about rapid social change and the coming millennium, hysteria should be on the increase. Each of the six syndromes which are the focus of the third part of the book is distinctive - but they are not discrete. Each develops according to a similar process of amplification and there is constant slippage between them. Indeed, it is Showalter's argument that it is the whole of contemporary American culture which is affected: 'when ... mass hysterias target enemies, when they develop links with religious fundamentalism, political paranoia or apocalyptic panic, they can turn into witch hunts or pogroms' (24).

The Female Malady concluded with an optimistic call for a feminist therapeutics. *Hystories* is deeply critical of some of the directions this has taken - for example, the use of hysteria itself as a rallying cry for feminism (feminism as a kind of articulate hysteria), and the putting on to a pedestal of the nineteenth century 'hysterical divas'. More important is the unquestioning endorsement by some feminists of abuse narratives such as Recovered Memory Syndrome and Satanic Abuse, and their accumulation of accusations, scape goating and conspiracy. The apparent cumulative effect of these, paradoxically, is to endorse rather then challenge many of the assumptions embedded in the history of hysteria. Showalter does not deny that real suffering is being experienced and expressed, but wants to ask alternative questions about the sources of these anxieties and sufferings, questions which are closed off by these conspiratorial therapeutic approaches as she sees them. We need to find more constructive ways of addressing these needs if we are to halt rather than succumb to the epidemic of suspicion and blame that threatens us all at the end of our centure (11).

Showalter's thesis is bold and complex. It proposes a general account of hysterical epidemics as a cultural phenonemon. The scope of her argument is broad, universalising hysteria in a political strategy which questions a feminist politics based on the historical synonymity between hysteria and women. This is a 'risky' strategy. Its strength is that, through the subtle expansion of the category of hysteria, it imposes a kind of explanatory order on very diverse and problematic contemporary phenomena. The 'problem' is that the shift to culture may collapse into one several phenomena which are in fact very different. Each of the six syndromes she deals with could have been the subject of a separate monograph. Another issue is whether the language of epidemic, plague and contagion which Showalter employs may have the effect of reporducing and amplifying the very phenomenon she challenges - representing part of the problem, rather than its solution. Nevertheless Showalter continues to be one of the few theorists capable of sensitising us to new dimensions of hysteria, which she sees as part of the psychopathology of everyday life: 'Whenever I lecture about hysteria, I cough. French psychoanalyst André Green, an internationally honoured member of the Freudian community, has joked that "we are all hysterics...except when we are writing papers"'.

Any honest scholar knows that we are all hysterics, *especially* when we are writing papers.

Dreams of the Promised Land

Sandra Bewick

Caryl Phillips, *The Nature Of Blood*, Faber, £15.99, 214 pp

'Tell me, what will be the name of the country?' asks a young Romanian boy in Cyprus. 'Israel' replies his companion. 'Our country will be called Israel'. Caryl Phillips' sixth novel begins here, in a Displaced Persons camp after the Second World War. Dr Stern, a man who has left his family to fight for a 'homeland', speaks to one of those waiting to be sent to Palestine: 'The fruit is on the trees', he tells the boy. 'You may take it straight from the branch'. The hunger for a Promised Land gnaws at the stomach of *The Nature of Blood*. Fragmented stories, broken and incomplete like the subjects who narrate them and the histories they evoke, cut precariously across one another in the uneasy space between a shimmering dream and its tragic realisation. This is a novel of little comfort.

Boldly resisting the boundaries of time and space, Phillips flies between pre-war Europe and Renaissance Venice, London, Cyprus, Israel. There is a preoccupation with history and always the 'violence of memory', as his displaced figures struggle to exist in worlds where the ambivalent fantasies of difference are realised as historic event. Eva, a young Jewish girl, meets her liberation from a concentration camp with crushing despair. She clutches to the memory of a familial space, but can no longer imagine 'home', a place where 'one feels a welcome'. An unnamed Othello haunts the city of Venice by gondalier, lonely, watchful, waiting. 'My friend, an African river', he recalls, 'bears no relation to a Venetian canal'. Three Jews from the ghetto of Portobuffolo are charged, condemned and executed for the sacrifice of a young Christian boy. Servadio, 'the chief conspirator', continues to pray as he climbs the scaffold in St Mark's Square. The desire to rest, to be, to belong, finds no satisfaction in Phillips' novel, where desolate narratives edge along a precipice of longing.

Phillips dances with the conventions of narrative, stumbling on occasion only to take a breath and start again elsewhere. Leaving aside the constraints of his own body, he glides provocatively through the psychic worlds of his protagonists, questions the nature of identification, frustrates attempts to hold him still. His rhythm is awkward and resistent, his prose both naked and clipped. Only during Othello's lonely travels through the dank and seductive lagoons of Venice does the language relax, a shift that feels almost indulgent when cut through by the stark phrasing of Eva's breakdown. Phillips makes his reader work, and it is not always an easy task.

There is little hope, despite the chinks of light that come from nowhere in the forms of love, compassion and sympathy. Othello's tale remains incomplete, his passion for Desdemona left to a fate already told. Eva is shown kindness by a British soldier, but it is a momentary friendship which ends in tragedy. Suffering and isolation are coupled here, unspeakable memories and unknown fears shatter the possibilities of a lasting comfort in another - 'There is no companionship in despair'. It is sometimes hard to reconcile these moments with the insistent reticence of Phillips' prose and the severed structures of his narratives. We are left outside, frighteningly disengaged from the 'obscene selfishness' of survival and the bleak landscapes of hopelessness. A final glimpse of Israel ends the novel, where a lonely, aging Dr Stern shares a moment of intimacy with Malka, an Ethiopian Jew, whose black skin is no longer welcome. Their shared dreams of 'home' are shattered by guilt, grief, isolation and a tragic sense of unbelonging. They have one night, but in the morning she has gone and he is left only with memory, 'a form of madness'.

Phillips is fascinated by histories of diaspora, by the world as it has been shaped by slavery, migration, the Holocaust and the politics of blood. His commitment to the interrogation of identity as a thing of imaginative possibilities is evident, and yet he consistently produces figures whose movements are determined by the structures of difference in which they are held. There remains a tension then, between the creative desire to refuse fixture, and the compulsion to work within historical constraints. Phillips is a restless writer, resisting solutions at every turn. He has his own story of migrancy, settlement, flight, and it is no surprise to find him with the displaced and forgotten, struggling with memory, 'that untidy room with unpredictable visiting hours', and the politics of 'home'. *The Nature of Blood* leaves us with uneasy questions about the nature of political identities and identifications, about a politics of articulation and action. Phillips suggests there is no place of rest; one can only look back to move forward, travel on to glance back, pause, briefly, until the wandering and the writing begins again.

'Young Britain'

INTRODUCTION

'Young Britain'

Jonathan Rutherford

> We will change the old and dead culture of Tory Britain.
>
> Tony Blair

Last summer, I was waiting for a bus at King's Cross in London. It was the day of a tube strike and there was a fractious air of impatience amongst the people waiting for the inevitably late bus. In the midst of the growing crowd, the bus shelter was empty. I looked inside. A young boy was lying fast asleep on a piece of cardboard, covered by an old grey blanket. His finger nails were rimmed with dirt, his hands filthy. He'd taken off his trainers and they were neatly placed beside his head. He was about fifteen to seventeen years old and oblivious to the crowd which massed around him. Nobody entered the shelter. People knew he was there, but had tacitly established a perimeter fence, a cordon sanitaire between themselves and the boy. An older man, drunk and semi-stupified, stopped as if he was going to enter and break the invisible boundary. As he swayed across the threshold it seemed tantamount to a physical assault and I realised that the crowd's refusal to make any claim on the bus shelter was not simply a fear of being assaulted or contaminated, but a way of protecting the boy and honouring him with a little dignity. The old man just looked and then walked off. The squalid, litter strewn space remained still and quiet; a teenager's surrogate bedroom at the bottom of the heap.

In 1988, Nicholas Scott, then minister for social security, withdrew social security benefits for 16 and 17 year olds. He took his cue from tabloid stories of unemployed youth living it up in an endless round of South Coast boarding houses: 'It is not the government's job to give an incentive to people to leave home.' By 1996, his peevish action had succeeded in making destitute thousands of young people. The Children's Society estimate that 50,000 young people, most

aged about fifteen, the majority escaping abuse, run away from home each year.
Shelter recently reported a disturbingly high proportion of 16 and 17 year olds
amongst the homeless callers to its emergency night line. During the summer of
1996, 8000 young people leaving local authority care were threatened with this
netherworld. 75 per cent had no academic qualifications. Between 50 per cent
and 80 per cent were jobless. One in seven of the young women were pregnant
or already mothers. 30 per cent of them will end up homeless.[1] The 1990s have
witnessed the deepening and extension of the deregulated market, the decline
of welfare and the growth of the anti-democratic state. This small minority of
young homeless bear the remorseless logic of these developments: deserted by
the state, family destroyed, without qualifications, without cultural capital, their
labour no longer a commodity of any value; there is little left but the intertwined
economies of prostitution, drugs and crime.

In 1995 Centaur Marketing ran their annual conference 'Targeting The Youth
Market' at the Cafe Royal in London. The central question before the assembled
delegates was 'Can the youth market be successfully targeted by socio-economic
background?' The long and the short of it was that it could not. In his presentation,
John Grant, planning director of St Luke's advertising agency, argued that a singular
youth culture which could be defined by its socio-economic location no longer existed.
The 16-24 year old generation was very difficult to define or divide into coherent
categories. There was diversity, there was difference, there were markets within
markets, there was a fluidity of identities which were in the continuous process of
being redefined. He argued it was much easier to describe the ingredients of their
culture than to describe *them*. He quoted the Henley Centre: one third of all 15-24
year olds claim to have been to a rave. Rave culture has touched the lives of more
under-25s than all previous youth cultures put together. But try and categorise 'rave'
and it fragments into a variety of sub-texts. Forget the style tribes, forget categories,
said Grant, use signifiers, use culture; target the young through their varying, virtual
connections to the media; grab them as *Loaded* readers, fans of *Friends* or the *X
Files*. Consumerism has played a pivotal role in creating youth cultural identities.
But here too today's generation of 16-24 year olds are a tricky commercial proposition.
The global market place has transformed youth cultures and their signs of revolt and

1. See *Too Much Too Young - The Failure of Social Policy in Meeting the Needs of Care
Leavers*, Barnados, London 1996.

rebellion into commodities, and an aesthetic of 'youth'. And youth cultural commodities are no longer confined to young people. It becomes hard to separate out the 'authentic' attributes of youth; but advertisers are in the business of freezing the cavalcade of street aspirations, pleasures and identities into instantly recognisable sound bites and images, long enough to commodify an aspirational identity and attach it to a product. This attempt to define 'youth' has become a perennial problem, as youth cultures fragment, metamorphose or become parodies of themselves.

If young people are presenting the marketplace with a complex game over how it can extend the process of commodification, they are also an unknown quantity to psephologists, political pundits and career politicians. 18-25 year olds make up 14.7 per cent of the UK electorate. In the 1992 election 2.5 million of this age group did not vote. No one is quite sure how they have responded in 1997; but nearly one in five young people are not even on the electoral register. New Labour, with its fascination for marketing strategies and focus groups and with its own profound cultural and political separation from young people, has attempted the advertiser's strategy. In his speech to the 1995 Labour Party Conference, Tony Blair made an appeal to this 'lost generation' by talking about the preoccupations of his own generation.

> Let me talk to you about my generation ... We were born into the Welfare State and the NHS, into the market economy of bank accounts, supermarkets, jeans and cars. We had money in our pockets never dreamt of by our parents ... We built a new popular culture, transformed by colour tv, Coronation Street and the Beatles. We enjoy a thousand material advantages over any previous generation; and yet we suffer a depth of insecurity and spiritual doubt they never knew.

Blair represented his generation as 'frightened for our future', living in 'a new age but in an old country'. In a rhetorical flourish he called for the rebirth of Britain. 'I want us to be a young country again. Young.'

Blair's clarion call for a young Britain follows the long romance of British radicalism with youth. But in the 1990s the myth of a golden age of youth has become tarnished. It's not just due to the hard times of young people, or any greater sobriety on their part. The jaundiced outlook belongs to those of Blair's generation who were formed by the political and cultural ideals of '1968'. A sense of political defeat has given many a more pessimistic outlook on the possibilities of social change, and the political and cultural potential of today's young. For some, the young are the products of Thatcherism and consumer culture: apolitical, their attention spans limited to three minutes, pursuing individual ambition to the detriment of social solidarity. The late 1980s marked the advent of a significant political and cultural gap between generations. The politics of *Marxism Today*, the legacies of libertarian socialism, feminism and Gramsci appear to have made little impact on today's young. Young people are not using the same political languages as their parents. Major innovations in music (techno, drum and bass) and computer technologies, the pervasiveness of the media in the lives of young people, the emergence of social purity movements around animal rights and environmentalism, plus a general 'feel bad factor' about Politics (with a capital P) have contributed to this generation gap. They have moved camp; they've gone somewhere else, currently off the political perceptual map of the older generation.

British capitalism has been undergoing a modernisation which is transforming its economic structure and its class culture and consciousness. Amongst the young, traditional work-based solidarities which once defined personal identity have been superseded by identities defined by consumption, lifestyles and leisure activities. The deregulation of the labour market and the decline of full-time male employment, together with the expansion of part-time female work, have contributed to an individualisation of society. Traditional forms of class and gender consciousness have been disrupted as people have been freed from traditional class and gender role prescriptions. Individualisation has not ended class as an organising category of capitalism, rather it has fragmented class cultural consciousness and consequently undermined the old forms of political mobilisation. There now exists a new sense of personal autonomy and individual choice, but it is curtailed by the massive increase in economic inequality and by new forms of institutional regulation. In 1979, 6 per cent of households had neither adult partner working. Today the figure is just under 20 per cent. The 1996 Rowntree Foundation *Inquiry into Income and Wealth* reported that the numbers living on less than half of average incomes had trebled since 1978. This polarisation has followed the fault lines of race and geographic location, and the summary impact has been disproportionately felt by the young. 60 per cent of 15-24 year olds have a disposable income of less than £50 per week.[2]

2. See *Never had it so good? The truth about being young in 90s Britain*, The British Youth Council, Barnados, London 1996.

In 1996 16-25 year olds constituted 13.3 per cent of the population. They made up 17 per cent of the workforce (compared to 23 per cent in 1986) and 35 per cent of the long term unemployed. In the summer of the same year, Youthaid reported that 142,000 school leavers were unemployed, taking the total of youth unemployment to 600,000. The main governmental response has been to expand and reform training and education provision. Despite a freezing of student numbers and a growing reluctance amongst the young to be saddled with the burden of debt and the uncertainties of the graduate jobs market, almost one third now enter higher education, compared to 1 in 7 in 1987. For the rest - the majority who have had the least opportunities in education - employment prospects are confined to the non-unionised sectors of catering, retailing and services. Here they experience an unrestrained version of the new managerial ethos in which the worker shoulders the risks and insecurities of the company's market performance. As Ian Brinkley writes in this issue of Soundings, the Tory mantra that people should follow the logic of the market and price themselves into jobs has proved false. The unemployment position of young people has worsened in the 1990s, despite substantial cuts in their relative pay. A survey carried out in 1994 by the Labour Research Department (commissioned by the GMB) reported that 30 per cent of jobs offered to young people yielded a net income below the income support threshold. 50 per cent offered between £3 and £4 per hour. Only 10 per cent of jobs offered any form of training. Without education and the acquisition of cultural capital - and even they provide no guarantees - the future offers only the insecurities of unemployment or working poverty. School has now become the site of new forms of class struggle as social classes compete for best entry positions into the employment market. It is a struggle inflected by race and gender relations.

Growing evidence suggests that white, working-class boys are at the bottom of the educational system. Statistics released by the Department of Education in 1995 show that 37 per cent of boys are achieving five or more A-C GCSE grades compared to 45.9 per cent of girls. In contrast, 50 per cent of young black eighteen year olds are still in full-time education, compared with 30 per cent of whites. However the rise of school exclusions in England - from 3000 in 1990 to over 11,000 in 1993 - contains a disproportionate number of black boys, presaging the very high rates of unemployment amongst young black men (see the Runnymede Trust's *True Stories and Pressures in Brixton* 1996). The picture is complex, and, despite the problems facing young black men, young people from ethnic minorities are now relatively over-represented in higher education. Young black and Asian women are doing the best of all, suggesting that they are using education as a strategy for gaining social inclusion.[3] There are plenty who believe that the superior educational performance of girls signals a more egalitarian gender culture and the redundancy of feminist battles for equality. However, their expectations have not been matched by changes in the structures of gender inequality. The educational achievements of young women and the time and energy invested in their education too often end in discrimination, disappointment and frustration in the labour market.

Individualisation has freed young women from the old gendered expectations of motherhood and homemaking. At the heart of post-war consumer capitalism in the 1950s, the middle-class family was a world where nature still appeared to determine one's destiny. But by the 1960s the capitalist market had begun to undermine the social form of the nuclear family. The new ideologies of individual choice contradicted women's fate as wives and mothers and exacerbated the tension between the structures of gender inequality and the growing consciousness of female autonomy. By the end of the 1960s the gendered relations of many, particularly middle-class, families were beset by an intense ambivalence over the role of women and the nature of femininity. In contrast, the invasion of modernity into the family had reinforced men's traditional role in the family. The sexual revolution encouraged the expansion of male heterosexual autonomy and personal status without any accompanying change in the structures of gender inequality: the domestic division of labour remained intact, men continued to monopolise full time wage labour, and the market and institutions privileged them over women. But women's growing consciousness that choice rather than fate could determine their lives delegitimised the ideologies of male authority. Masculine roles and behaviours were increasingly challenged. For boys, the ambivalence of the mother, and her perception of his father as a man lacking empathy with her, reinforced the already existing gulf between father and son. The decline of female gender fate enabled girls to acquire a greater degree of independence from the prescribed roles of their mothers; but conversely it had the effect of reinforcing boys' identification with their mothers.

Despite a loosening identification with traditional male roles, men were still

---

3. See Heidi Safia Mirza's argument about young black women's strategies to succeed at school, in *Education Today and Tomorrow*, Vol 49 No1 Spring 1997, and in *Black British Feminism*, Heidi Safia Mirza (ed), Routledge, London 1997.

relatively free of social and economic contradictions until the onset of unemployment and deindustrialisation in the 1980s. Even then men remained relatively uninterested in the predicaments of their gender identities. Men experienced the central conflicts of modernisation through women. Women prompted change in the private realm of parenting, sexuality, emotions and psychological well-being; precipitating personal crises for men and a recognition of their emotional dependency on women. For the grandchildren of the 1960s, this changing dynamic of gender relations has profoundly shaped their own response to the new uncertainties of the 1990s. Young women appear to have a greater social confidence.

'Ineptitude in interpersonal skills so often passes for appropriate masculine behaviour'

The legacy of feminism has been a transformation in their attitudes and aspirations. In contrast to young women's ambition to succeed, while young men still maintain a gendered privilege, many appear to be floundering. Individualisation coupled with the massive rise in male redundancy and the increasing numbers of women in employment have undermined the old rules and roles and they can no longer expect an allotted place in society. The scorn for the feminised work of education and mental skills amongst many young working-class men suggests they have failed to recognise the technological revolution which is transforming the nature of men's work. But their self-deception is part of their fear of failing to match the social confidence, interpersonal skills and intellectual dexterity of the young women. Divested of hope and a productive role in society, unable to achieve adult independence, and unwilling to contribute to the domestic economy of their mothers' homes, many young men have simply given up.

Male redundancy has created cultures of prolonged adolescence in which young male identities remain locked into the locality of estate, shops and school. Violence, criminality, drug taking and alcohol consumption become the means to gaining prestige for a masculine identity bereft of any social value or function. A 1996 Home Office report, *Young People and Crime*, based on 2500 interviews confirmed this prolongation of young men's anti-social adolescent behaviour. One half of the teenage boys and one third of the girls interviewed had been involved in crime. By their mid twenties young women have grown out of crime, only 4 per cent admitting to committing a crime other than drug taking. In contrast, the figure for men of a similar age was 31 per cent. Men were less likely to have left home, less likely to be in stable relationships and less likely to have secure employment. The researchers found only a weak link between crime and social class. The pattern of prolonged adolescence extends beyond areas of economic deprivation. Ineptitude in interpersonal skills, which so often passes for appropriate masculine behaviour, leaves young men ill-equipped to cope with social isolation and despair. In Britain, in 1982, according to the Office of Population Censuses and Statistics, 320 young men aged between 15 and 24 killed themselves. In 1992, the number was 500, an increase of 56 per cent. Young women too are under duress. Evidence of depression is twice as high amongst women while their incidence of 'suicidal behaviour' (as opposed to actual suicide) is also higher. Michael Rutter and David J. Smith in their 1996 report *Psychosocial Disorders in Young People* argue that this increase in mental ill-health is not a consequence of social and economic deprivation, but a result of the changing nature of adolescence and young people's isolation from the rest of society. It is perhaps young men who are most detached, socially and emotionally, from family life, following a trend which will see men under pensionable age as the largest category of single householders by the year 2011 (*Social Trends* 1996).

These vicissitudes, combined with the withdrawal of state support from young people, have made access to family support crucial. Youth unemployment and the increase in post-compulsory education have extended the period of young people's dependency on their parents (64 per cent of 16-24 year olds live with their parents). The Conservative government encouraged this trend and sought to institutionalise it in legislation. The Job Seekers Allowance, introduced in October 1996, is designed to keep unemployed people under twenty-four at home with their parents and confirms the state's attempt to use the family as an institution of labour discipline and social order. Young people have suffered the most severe cuts to their benefit. Single 18-24 year olds lose £10 per week (a loss of £540 per year) under the new scheme, forcing them to rely on their families for financial support and creating intolerable stresses amongst the poor and badly paid. The JSA intensifies pressure on the unemployed to take low paid work. By requiring them to develop a personal employability plan it shifts the responsibility for unemployment onto the moral and personal conduct of the individual. In the context of pluralised underemployment and a 'disorganised' labour market, the effect is to blur the boundary between being in work and being out of work. Unemployment as a linguistic concept ceases to exist. The effect is to drive thousands of young people off benefit and out of the mainstream economy altogether, either into an indefinite dependency on their families or into illicit forms of money making. Enforced economic dependency takes away young people's cultural, social and personal autonomy and denies them any semblance of citizenship. It is this antagonism between the cultural expectations of the young and the inability of the economic system to realise them that has been the major source of youth unrest and the principal site of the state's political intervention in young people's lives.

Since the 1980s New Right social reformers, intellectuals and politicians have challenged the existence of any social presumption of young people's rights to self determination. Their ambition has been to regenerate the discursive machinery which has defined and regulated 'the adolescent' and 'youth' (criminal justice system, civil and family law, schooling, employment and social security legislation). In 1986, David Marsland, in a melodramatically entitled essay 'Young People Betrayed', written for the right-wing think tank The Social Affairs Unit, called for the restoration of the family's responsibility for young people.[4] He argued that society should stop treating young people as if they were adults and recognise their need for caring support and firm leadership. His first concern was the tide of divorce, which had to be reversed through changes in attitudes and in the legal and procedural frameworks which he believed made divorce 'far too common and far too easy'. Next, the monopoly of the liberal educational establishment over young people's lives should be removed by handing responsibility for education back to parents. And the grants system in further and higher education - which enabled young people to pursue 'inappropriate studies' and led to their 'bewitchment' 'by the pied pipers of campus peer groups' - should also be controlled by parents. Parents could retain control over their student offspring by being responsible for financing them through college, aided by a system of loans. Finally, Marsland proposed the removal of all rights to benefit for the unemployed young. By the 1990s his cranky aspirations for the regulation of young people were either in effect or had moved to the centre of political debate. The New Right's ambition to reestablish the patriarchal family as a form of social cohesion and to promote the figure of the

---

4. David Marsland, 'Young People Betrayed', in *Full Circle? Bringing up Children in the Post-Permissive Society*, Digby Anderson (ed), Social Affairs Unit, London 1988.

father as a symbol of cultural authority in what it perceived to be an increasingly 'adolescent' society is no longer the staple attitude of the Tory right alone.

In 1995 John Redwood blamed the soaring welfare budget on 'too many young women ... having babies and 'marrying' the state. Too many unmarried young men ... walking away from their responsibilities as fathers' (News of the World, 17 September 1995). By the mid-1990s this kind of moralising rhetoric had become common parlance amongst the governing classes of all the political parties. Social democrats, seeking to locate the unmanageable macro-problems of social dislocation in what they believed to be the manageable personal behaviours of individuals had adopted Amitai Etzioni and his idea of communitarianism. Etzioni offered a link between liberalism and the new politics of social discipline by making the Victorian, imperial language of character building respectable again: 'Character formation lays the psychic foundation for the ability both to mobilise to a task and to behave morally by being able to control impulses and defer gratification.'[5] The emphasis on the personal regulation of moral conduct as a conservative response to social exclusion has been evident in the technocratic transformation of the Labour Party as it accommodates the deregulated market economy. Its policy approach to the young has much in common with old Victorian improving organisations, like the Boy's Brigade, which disseminated the ideals and practices of the public school's religion of character-building in an attempt to bring social discipline to the working classes. Peter Mandelson and Roger Liddle, promoting their book The Blair Revolution - Can New Labour Deliver? in The Guardian (27 February 1996) were succinct in their no-nonsense carrot and stick approach:

Britain urgently needs to put in place a new contract between society and young people ... to help young people find a sure footing in the adult world, but with tough penalties for those who refuse the opportunity and fail to fulfil their side of the bargain.

In defence of its politics of social discipline, New Labour cite the language of citizen's rights and responsibilities. But their version of citizenship does not guarantee social and economic equality and, without a determined effort to tackle the injustices of inequality, it is a rhetoric which betrays an authoritarian, bullying streak, with the

5. Amitai Etzioni, 'Learning Right from Wrong', in Demos Quarterly, Issue 1, Winter, 1993.

easier targets of the poor and powerless coming in for the most moral condemnation. In some respects New Labour has become the political technocrat's version of old labourism; paternalism replaced by the new managerialism, and a continuing suspicion of social movements and autonomous democratic politics. Blair's political revolution has principally been couched in the language of a new puritanism: a pilgrimage toward a 'decent society'. In the months before the election its moral earnestness concerned itself less with a passion for social justice, and more with an ambition for political power. Inevitable perhaps, but the rhetorical strategies of pre-election New Labour, in particular of Tony Blair and Jack Straw, tailored for the fictitious middle England, simply reproduced the family values and disciplinary politics of the Conservatives. New Labour's emphasis on focus groups and marketing strategies has been symptomatic of a political order which has closed itself off from the culture and emotions of democratic change. In the face of the 'first past the post' electoral system and a hostile press, the logic of all of this may appear irrefutable. But in the longer term this neglect of what should be the central strands of any regenerative politics - pleasure, pluralism, inclusiveness, hope - may simply serve to deaden the idealism which first surrounded Blair when he became the leader of the Labour Party, and the euphoria of the Labour landslide.

Blair is a paradox. His rhetoric reverberates with the symbolic significance of youth. His own relative youthfulness and his winsome good looks evoke the myth of Kennedy's Camelot. His courtiers exude an ambition and 'nowness' that comes with the promise of power. But his pilgrim's progress is old fashioned and garnered from a religious morality of service and duty. It leads him inexorably back to an imaginary middle England which his own father inhabits and where he grew up. Blair is right that middle England holds the political key to the future of Britain. It is the dominant imaginary representation of white English ethnicity. But the middle England of the late 1990s, which was fashioned a decade ago by Thatcherism, and which appeared to hold him in its thrall, had nothing to offer but its own, often rancorous disappointments. Middle England can be future oriented and young in spirit. It could be part of a new democratic and constitutional settlement: open to differences of sexuality and race, less class bound, not hemmed in with fear of foreigners, nor obsessed with proper family arrangements, or selfish concern for itself. It already contains the seeds of these changes, particularly within the younger generation. But it has to be imagined, and then it has to be believed in, and the question mark next to

Blair's rhetoric of the 'new' is whether or not he can believe in his own words.

Blair is ambivalent about his own youth. He belongs to a generation of men less convinced about their masculine authority than their fathers were. Men who have had a closer identification with their mothers and who have always felt in the shadow of their fathers. Faced with a generation of fathers in political power - in the civil service, in the military, in industry and business, even in his own party - Blair has manufactured a manly authority and certitude. Associations with youth, with its connotations of inexperience, irresponsibility and immaturity, were a threatening prospect in his pursuit of political power. Watching Blair head a football with Kevin Keagan was to see a man determined to prove himself. The pleasure, even the point of it, was secondary. Blair still feels himself a son amongst fathers, anxious about measuring up. There is a photograph of him wearing jeans, relaxed in a chair, strumming an electric guitar. It signifies informality, youthfulness - a man who grew up in the youth culture of the 1960s. But behind him, placed prominently on a table, is a large picture of himself and Cherie Booth. The picture overlays the image of youth and signifies his adult status of heterosexual, married father. The juxtaposition in this photographic image says a great deal about Blair's own personal insecurities. These are most evident in his dealings with popular culture. He is more at home with the aspirational language of success and service to a cause, than with pleasure and desire. Yet it is in popular culture, the place young people inhabit, that Blair must conduct a dialogue with youth, and make his pitch for their support.

I f he and New Labour choose to listen, they'll find a generation where there are sophisticated opinions and untapped ideals. As Elaine Pennicott argues in her piece about the new black British popular fiction, young black Britons, despite their exclusion from the mainstream, are engaged in important and creative ways with the cultural life of this country. Similarly, Bilkis Malek's essay on young British Asians suggests no hint of cultural or political inertia on their part. But here are two social groups whose cultural and social visibility is still confined to stereotypical images. Despite their strong presence in higher education, their reservoir of talent, ambition and determination is still largely ignored. Peter Gartside's incisive look at the politics of eco-protests reveals an imaginative and innovative movement which has become deeply politicised by the Criminal Justice Act. This is a generation which shares a common apathy toward Westminster's brand of politics. As Mike Kenny describes in 'That's

Entertainment', the need to establish connections between young people and the political community is an apparently intractable problem for modern states. Youth cultures are fashioned out of the market and popular culture, not through the civic discourses of democratic politics, and they find no representation in the preoccupations and language of a culturally homogeneous, self-referential party politics. Young people today lack defined political identifications with which to communicate collective hopes and grievances. This absence of institutionalised forms of representation, combined with the social exclusion and impoverishment of large sections of young people, is creating a crisis of democracy.

Where the media has represented an identifiable politics within the 16-24 generation - DIY and eco-protest - its character has been fundamentally antagonistic to the culture and ethos of New Labour. In contrast to New Labour's image of a party of capitalist modernisation, these politics have often turned to anti-modern, anti-rationalist values. Young people have been at the forefront of counter cultures, searching for the reenchantment of contemporary life in the mediaeval communities of travellers, animal rights, the mysticism of paganism and tree-huggers and the holistic rhetoric of rave culture. As Peter Gartside argues, it is a politics which is simultaneously here and not here - ephemeral, transient, disorganised. Divining the attitudes and values of this generation has meant looking to their cultural, artistic and musical expression. As Rupa Huq shows in 'Paradigm Lost?', it is here that the nascent political languages and sensibilities of the new generation are taking shape. She cites the example of the extraordinary rise of the Spice Girls as a symbol of the sexual confidence of 'girl power' - a popular cultural expression of youthful aspirational femininities which has had no representation in civic or political life.

New Labour in power must win a cultural hegemony which will help secure its hold on the British state. The energy, innovation and idealism of young people are central to achieving this task. Not only can a new generation transform the cultural, gendered and ethnic meanings of Middle England; its political commitment will also help secure Labour a second term in office. New Labour has to foster ideological connections between the cultures and activities of young people and a democratising state. Instead of trying to co-opt young people into its own political machinery it has to develop a dialogue with them. This means listening to and learning from the sounds and images coming from youth cultures, ending the prescriptive, hectoring tone inherited from communitarianism, and developing a politics which encourages the political and cultural aspirations of young people. Jonathan Keane's essay on Ecstasy puts forward a persuasive image of a generation that is both idealistic and disenchanted; one which has created a drug culture that has become 'an ode to lost joy'. The fear and silence amongst politicians around the issue of drugs serves only to increase youthful cynicism with politicians and adults in general. We need a return to idealism, and that requires risk-taking and innovation on the part of political leaders. The TUC's New Unionism is about developing a political culture of organising which will depend on the collective idealism of young people for its success. John Healey and Frances O'Grady write about an initiative which is rooted in the experiences of the early civil rights workers in the deep South of the United States, the American peace corps, and our own Community Service Volunteers. New Labour in government must also construct initiatives for its own regeneration and long term survival. A powerful gesture to begin with would be the introduction of a £4 minimum wage. It would send a clear and bold message to young people that politics can make a real difference to their lives. They might then listen. A conversation might begin.

The purpose of this 'Young Britain' issue of Soundings is to encourage dialogue across the generations and to create an opportunity to explore the nature of generational differences, similarities and connections. At the same time I hope it makes a small contribution toward constructing political and cultural languages which speak to and about young people. In this respect it is part of a growing response to the political and economic predicaments of young people. There have been significant changes and differences between the radical politics generated in the 1970s (class, anti-racism, feminism, gay liberation) and the radical politics of the 1990s. But as George McKay has shown in his book Senseless Acts of Beauty (Verso 1996), continuity has existed in the politics and practices of the counterculture, dating back to the hippy free festivals of the 1960s, on through punk sub cultures to present day eco-radicals and young people's resistance to the Criminal Justice Act. Equally there has been a continuity in what I can only call the ordinariness of people's lives - the aspirations for love, a good life, useful, properly paid employment, pleasure and happiness. Young people today are faced with a qualitatively different society from the one their parents grew up in. Their political economy reveals a great deal about the ongoing restructuring of British capitalism and its class system, just as their cultures of resistance reflect the current strengths and weaknesses of radical democratic politics.

PROTEST
THE ILLEGALITY OF NUCLEAR WEAPONS

CAMPAIGN
AGAINST ALL WEAPONS OF GENOCIDE

JOIN US on a cycle tour of some of Southern England's military and nuclear sites. There will be peace camps open to all* when we stop at each site - come and show your support.

WHAT YOU CAN DO:

We'd like as many women as possible to cycle all or part of the route

Meet us at the peace camps we'll be setting up each evening along the route

Raise sponsorship £££ for local groups working on issues of radiation

THE ROUTE: Aug 8-10 - *Aldermaston*; Aug 11 - *Harwell*; Aug 12 - *Farnborough*;
Aug 13 - *Royal Naval Dockyard*, Portsmouth; Aug 14-16 - *Burghfield*.

For more information contact Helen, 33 Heron Road, Bristol BS5 0LT.

* women only overnight

CELEBRATION ENTERTAINMENTS

QUALITY ENTERTAINERS FOR PARTIES, FESTIVALS & CONFERENCES

To make your party or event extra special contact Celebration Entertainments for interesting, reliable, professional artists.

Celebration Entertainments offer a wide choice of acts, from poetry readers to a gospel choir.

Entertainers include: story tellers, alternative comedians, tarot card readers, jugglers, clowns, magicians, a variety of musicians, including a string quartet; and actors for short plays and theme work. We also have an inspiring range of children's entertainers.

Celebration Entertainments will happily provide function helpers and advise on caterers and venues.

Contact: Nikki Williams on 0181 245 5338

Ecstasy in the unhappy society

Jonathan Keane

Jonathan Keane *looks at contemporary youth's most popular anti-depressant.*

THE UNHAPPY SOCIETY: A PEOPLES HISTORY

CHAPTER 9
THE FREE MARKETEERS
(OR WAITING FOR THE FEEL GOOD FACTOR)

Throughout 1996 British economic indicators appeared extraordinarily favourable. Inflation was at an all time low. There was an expanding economy and unemployment was falling faster than in any of the countries of the old European Empire. The ruling Tory executive welcomed this new age of prosperity. Yet they were uneasy. They could not comprehend why the public were not feeling good.

They viewed British citizens as simple souls. Their actions and pleasures nothing more than a series of rational economic choices. They also believed that their policies had enabled those choices to be made as efficiently, and so pleasurably, as possible. The British people thus had no reason to be unhappy. Yet the Conservatives failed to understand that the British people were not wholly rational.

To achieve their aims the Conservatives had deregulated the labour market. Unfettered by corporate regulation, they believed people would respond to changes in the economy like any good price sensitive product of the period: their wage prices going up and down when necessary; their working hours following suit.

People were straightjacketed into economically correct personalities and placed under relentless pressure to be productive. Workplaces thus became surreal environments where employees had to learn to behave and think in a limited way: a repetitive masquerade of treating the customer right, of dressing correctly and of doing increasingly simplistic tasks. Satisfaction for customer and employee alike thus became illusory. Relations between them ordered by a logic beyond their control: the desire to create super profit for its own sake. These circumstances led to an increase in psychological disorders across the whole spectrum of working experience.

Not content with reorganising business so that it would run for its own sake, the Conservative Party set upon public life. They let the market organise home life, education, service provision and even the social spaces where people conducted relationships. Within this environment people were not free to develop their own sense of identity and they became lost.

The most heinous consequence of this system was the effect it had on the development of the young. Children were placed under relentless pressure to be aware of the importance of schoolwork to their future prospects. They were tested and placed in tabular leagues at every age, forced to encounter the stress of adult reality even before they reached puberty.

Faced with an unstable labour market, the young's fantasies of a better life, so crucial to individual and social development, became stunted by short term anxieties. Discontented and demotivated, they began not to look forward at all. Instead they looked to buy their happiness in the immediacy of the consumer present. Leisure became their religion and, for a time, their saviour.

The general public were unhappy despite the apparent good state of the economy, because their well being had been the price for its success.

In the Year of Our Soul 3010

Happiness, the elusive British fantasy

Unhappiness is the cornerstone of our British national identity. Our emotional unconscious. In the present, we only dare talk of it in metaphorical terms; mythologising it as some intangible ability to withstand adversity such as the 'Great British Spirit'. We make of it a sign of positive strength. Yet in truth it is the cultural neurosis that stops us challenging those political objectives that cause discontent.

Once, the merits of day to day unhappiness were repetitively drilled into British culture by the dictates of the work ethic. Austere Puritan and calvinistic doctrine coursed through western economic discourse, business and corporate organisational structures. As workers and consumers within those organisations, they shaped our own desires, relationships and knowledge of self.

We remained unconscious of the fact because those same theologies promised future rewards that kept us away from the truth: if we were unlucky in the first life we would be rewarded in the second. And after the rise of industrial capital, if we worked hard we could, eventually, gain Heaven on Earth.

But the dreams of both God and work have lost their seductive allure in nineties Britain. The general public no longer believe in Heaven, and employment is no longer a stable enterprise that allows individuals to ignore their present and look forward to a happy retirement. With the breakup of these rational organising principles our unhappy unconscious is breaking through the cracks in wave after wave of sadness and discontent.

Drugs and me

I first took Ecstasy in March 1994 at Heaven, a gay nightclub in London. At the time, I was working in Waterstone's Booksellers on Kensington High Street. I was new to London, harassed by unfriendly staff and public alike, and only half living on a pitifully low wage.

I went to the club with my flat mate, a close friend. When we arrived she suggested that we drop some 'E'. I was really fed up, feeling isolated and trapped in a boring little world over which I felt I had no control so I thought what the hell and bought, bit and swallowed my way to what I hoped would be oblivion.

Nothing happened for a good half hour. We had taken half each, and with immediate cynicism I decided it hadn't been enough. I danced somewhat self consciously, eyes towards my feet.

Then a sensation. A warmness in my stomach that spread through my body.

After a few minutes I felt a tingling in my neck and then a splurge of gloriously happy energy, steeping my thoughts in an emotional blur of love and excitement. It was as if I were at a concert and music had washed over me with that delicate emotional frisson only some singers can produce, lifting me high. I was ready to slip back down into normality but found that each successive surge of warmth up my neck was taking me further into joy.

It was almost too much for me to take. I couldn't remember ever feeling that good. What was more surprising was that I could think with a freedom that I hadn't known before. I looked at my friend and was able to dismiss much of the normal flatmate angst one picks up when living with someone and see her for the wonderful friend that she was. I could dance in an unrestrictive way, feeling that my body would respond to anything I asked of it, and it did. I looked around and felt confident to search out the eyes of attractive men. It was as if I had been given an intuitive energy that allowed me to look at myself and my environment as it was, without fear, and know what I wanted from it.

The most significant part of the experience came later. A small door had opened in my life and I could see that I was trapping myself in an unhappy job and lifestyle, and that with a bit of work I could be happier. Perhaps not as happy as I felt on the drug, but at least more in touch with who I really was. Three months later I left my job and started on a new career path and the most wonderful relationship I have ever had.

The media's heady quest for youth

The middle classes and the middle aged feel unsettled about people that have taken Ecstasy. For them, it is a symbol of the unhappy society that they would like to ignore. So they shout angrily, punish as much as they are able, and do little to understand. Their torrent of guilty denial found a suitable totem in the memory of Leah Betts.

Leah was 18, at the start of her adult life. To celebrate she had a party and an ecstasy tablet. Tragically, she drank too much water. Her kidney could not push the excess fluid out of her system. Her brain swelled causing cerebral coning, and she fell into a permanent coma. Leah's mother was a nurse and a drugs counsellor, and her father used to work for the drugs squad, factors that leant a terrible pathos and symmetry to the context of her death.

Leah became a vehicle for a moral panic. Her face was pasted onto billboards in a nationwide campaign launched by advertising director Paul Delaney. The word 'Sorted' was written large in white on black caps underneath her smiling face. Below ran the warning, 'only one ecstasy tablet killed Leah Betts'.

The press reacted with a statistical scramble for figures and surveys, so that youth could be understood, contained and told the naughtiness of their ways. The *Independent on Sunday* ran a 'Real Life' supplement, anachronistically entitled 'Sex Drugs and Rock 'n' Roll'. They announced in a surprised tone that youth are taking drugs in a recreational capacity, 'not junkies on a slow decline into the gutter, not crazed radicals, [as parents would expect] but discerning consumers who decide exactly how much they take and how often'.

Throughout 1996 media youth anxiety bounced off any convenient cultural event; especially the films, *Kids*, *Trainspotting* and *Crash*. By the end of the year their chatter crystallised into a political debate on the containment of youth. Parent-teacher contracts were floated in the public arena and the Liberal and Labour Parties succeeded in banning certain knives following the murder of school head teacher Philip Lawrence. By early 1997 the confessions of a drug-taking popstar, 22 year old Brian Harvey, were deemed important enough to be addressed by John Major during prime minister's question time.

Youth became victim to the sensationalism that today directs the media's search for knowledge. They were depicted as monsters, alien to the normal world of the political and intellectual leaders of conservative Britain. It was as if the baby boomers who had created this B movie picture forced youth outside of their world view so they would not threaten their values.

Meanwhile young people laughed in the face of misunderstanding. As Thatcher's and Major's children, their identities have been formed in the epistemological free for all of the 1980s and 1990s. A time when nothing was true for very long. They have no outsides, no distance from life. As a result they are street wise, intelligent realists whom understand the fast pace of our society better than their parents. They knew that Leah's death was not happening to someone every weekend, because the majority had not seen it happen.

Youth culture and the flight of fantasy

In some respects youth baiting is not a new phenomenon. Ever since teenagers appeared on the cultural scene during the 1950s they have been viewed as troublesome. First came the mods and rockers, then 1960s flower children, 1970s punks and 1980s new romantics. Each generation with different clothes, hairstyles, pop idols, politics, and the clubs that gave their pubescent desires a temporary home.

Yet for most of the previous generations of young soul rebels, youth culture was a simple fantasy food, with a real world sell-by date. Being young was a series of learning games that led to the prize of emotional maturity and the more complete fantasies of adult life.

1980s and 1990s youth culture, however, is not ruled by the ephemeral logic of fantasy. Nor is it quickly consigned to personal history by fantasy's dogmatic partner, gross reality. The dynamism of the free market has put paid to that. Instead youth live in a hyper-real world where they can buy and sustain the look they want, the music they want, even the type of friends they want, by organising into a visible market segment. Those who cannot afford to do so respond with the same consumerist spirit and create their own complex street cultures and black markets.

In a society judged by market values, youth culture thus appears more abundant, more efficient, even more grown-up than an adulthood that still adheres to a corporatist logic of work and social responsibility. That world, with its economic uncertainties, its lack of fun and its inertia, fails to seduce the young. The hyper-real is larger than life and ultimately more alluring.

To remain seductive, this hyper-real culture must relentlessly recreate the illusion of new music, fashion and entertainment. Of course, as victims of the short-term anxieties of the market, producers have no time to create the actual new. Instead they recycle the culture of previous eras, and increasingly of the previous day, by simply adding a glossy spin.

Youth are consequently placed in the inert eye of a cultural tornado, and the abundance of goods and empty soundbite information that swirls around them becomes contradictory, confusing and evacuated of sense. Psychologically, youth are displaced and disorientated, relentlessly thrown up into the air by the promise of consumer fulfilment. A quick fix with an empty culture leaves them dazed and confused and flying back for more. Yet, like the Wizard of Oz, behind its impressive surface, this culture has no real stability or power to confer. Not even DNKY ruby slippers can magic the young back to somewhere that feels like home.

With their egos built on shifting cultural sands, the unhappy unconscious of the young breaks through. With it rises an anxious desire to find a new way of keeping dissatisfaction at bay. As politics has also been seduced by marketing spin it can offer only soundbite alternatives. Young individuals thus turn towards the only real thing they know and can control, their own bodies.

I'm ravin, I'm ravin

British rave culture is the quintessential body culture. The music played on the scene is a faceless rhythm and a soaring emotional litany into which the young immerse themselves. Rave was born around 1986 at the beginning of the monetarist boom. A cultural refuge from the chaotic storm of the 'me' decade. Acid House was then in the ascendant playing at underground parties. Today it is estimated that 100,000 young people go clubbing every week. Yet the young were never just interested in the music. In this age of extremes, escape strategies need a little help. Ecstasy answered the call.

The drug came to Britain around 1987 via psychotherapeutic and yuppie recreational use in the United States, and the dance culture of the holiday island of Ibiza. British holiday-makers saw its potential for their own dance scene and imported it. They probably never dreamed how popular it would become. Yet they had delivered something magical to our depressive country: happiness in tablet form.

Taking 'E' precipitates a surge of love and a feeling of well-being by acting on the brain to encourage excess production of the neurotransmitter serotonin. This canny nerve fluid acts as a sort of chemical e-mail link between the brain cells where our memories, feelings and emotions reside. It is also thought to regulate our general mood.

Under the influence, takers become ecstatically happy. At the same time their contradictory collection of thoughts, fears and neuroses become conscious and connected, yet not in repressive competition with each other. Like in Zen Buddhist meditation, a calm order rests on thought, and you see yourself as whole. In the buoyancy of this cerebral positivity you can empathise freely and warmly with other people.

The rave scene thus potentially creates an environment where bodies become sources of self knowledge and the ground for identity. A calm counter activity and a welcome relief from the empty chatter of the market culture.

I'm feeling a little different

It's like at a rave we create a kind of environment and it isnae just the E - that encourages that kind ay feelin. It's the whole vibe. But it doesnae transfer that well tae the ootside world. Oot thair, these cunts have created a different environment and that kind of environment lends itself mair tae the swedge rush.[1]

The guru of the Drug culture, Irvine Welsch, wrote in a short story called *Fortunes Always Hiding; A Corporate Drug Romance*. It is a story of aggressive lads, the football firm looking for a ruck before and after a soccer match. One character, Rigsie, used to be a good firm lad, but now he is more interested in love and dealing. He is a figure on the skirts of the macho frame of the story, upsetting the camaraderie of the boys and their little world of adrenalin-fuelled aggro and aggressive commonality with his absent peaceful vibe. In this tale weird love seeps in at the seams.

Time passes strangely in the land of 'E'. Your metabolism is speeded up because of the amphetamine in the drug and you feel more alive than usual. Add constant happiness and a background of music with no apparent beginning or end and you have the illusion of an endless present.

Within this timeless environment young men and women are finding the space to relate differently. The drug compels men to express themselves. Research has suggested that regular use produces lower serotonin levels in the brain. This, it is claimed, can lead to a decrease in indirect hostility and less impulsive and more harm avoidant behaviour. The jury is still out as to whether that indicates neurotoxic damage or glorious evolution - it is probably both. But could it be true that Ecstasy feminises the brain?

Perhaps, but, whatever future research concludes, it is true that some combination of physiological change and cultural influence is queering men up. They hug each other. They do not feel threatened by gay men, and, perhaps most importantly, they stop competing. Instead they form their identities in empathy with others. Not from being braver than their peers nor by having a women on their arm.

This is all good news for our heterosexist, macho culture culture. But it is also good for intimate relations between the sexes. Men find it difficult to get erections under the influence and they feel less actively sexy. The nub of phallocentricism happily losing both its cultural and physical grandeur. Both men and women then feel inclined to touch each other just for the intimacy of the experience. Women thus feel less threatened by men's sexuality and feel more in control of their own. While men feel less interested in the laddy rush to procure, shag and brag about

---

1. Irvine Welsch, *Ecstasy*, Jonathan Cape, London 1996, p260.

the trophy. Sex sessions on 'E' have been known to last for hours.

Of course one downside of the drug is that it also impairs judgment. When pissed on alcohol there is nothing worse than waking up next to someone you do not even recognise. In E culture you may wake up next to someone you thought was the love of your life, or of a different sex, only to find he is a dirty train spotter from Croydon. Not nice.

'E' has risen up like a bird in flight, a dove perhaps, a symbol frequently imprinted on the tablets themselves, and allowed young relationships to rest on a more humanistic plateau. Out of these utopian celebrations of self comes a feeling of commonality merged with individual pleasure on a scale that Marx believed would only come with the revolution.

Unfortunately, the breakdown of competitive masculinity is not something that conservative Britain feels inclined to embrace.

The rule of law

Between 1990 and 1994, the Tory government effectively criminalised young people in Britain. Firstly, the Entertainments (Acid House) Increased Penalty Act of 1990 made a criminal offence of holding unlicensed underground parties. This precipitated a twofold effect on the rave scene. Some groups and organisers linked up with the free festival circuit and other more money orientated organisers began to move into city centre clubs.

Outdoor raves such as that at Castlemorton in May 1992, played host to between 25,000 and 50,000 people. Old style hippy travellers and new age rave kids met here in a strange land of pleasure and self discovery away from the pressure of their normal lives. These free parties were the perfect environments for 'E' and other drug use. Cool, well facilitated, medical care on hand replete with conversation about philosophy and religion to help direct thoughts and discoveries emerging from the use of the drug.

The government reacted to this new noisy culture with the infamous 1994 Criminal Justice and Public Order Act and made illegal the very idea of rave, describing it in laughable phrases such as 'a gathering ... including a place partly in the open air'; it described rave music as a vague group of 'sounds which are wholly or predominantly characterised by a series of repetitive beats'. Unlicensed raves seemed dead on their stomping feet, as, ironically, did outdoor weddings.

Both the 1991 and 1994 Acts politicised many members of the dance culture and they concentrated their energies on creating their own anti-capitalist worlds. Drugs were a tool of insight to help form an alternative way of life

Today, DIY party culture is losing a war of attrition against the police powers granted by the 1994 Act, and their humanism has gone underground. Sometimes the vibe of that scene pops up in the odd warehouse party in London, or the odd out of town quarry. But this type of radical 'E' culture has fled so far from the mainstream that you have to have a degree in sociology and an orienteering qualification just to begin looking for it. For the majority, this culture is consigned to history.

Legalised drug markets

The type of 'E' culture that is still on the up after eight years is the licensed club scene. The various Conservative criminal justice Acts have unwittingly produced a marketised version of the original underground culture. This is especially true of London, where the number of techno, house, jungle and other music clubs, all tailored to a particular youth market segment, beggars belief.

Many clubs are highly dangerous; they lack sufficient air conditioning and do not provide access to free drinking water or chill out areas. The majority of the 60 odd deaths from ecstasy since 1990 have been caused by heatstroke brought on by this environment.[2] They are also heavily codified in terms of style. Where only the beautiful, affluent and fashionable are made to feel welcome.[3] Poorer youth often sacrifice other parts of their life or turn to a bit of dealing so that they can afford to join in.

The cultural tornado of the consumer world has been let loose in youth's drug intensified realm of experience, along with its addictive empty seduction and fashionable pretension. It dictates that the 'E' user must play out a role just to be a part of the scene. Yet, taking a drug that breaks down psychological barriers in an environment that, essentially, is trying to build them up can be extremely dangerous. The combination can cause anxiety and paranoia in the insecure, and, for some troubled individuals, a breakdown in relations with with reality.

---

2. Ecstasy confuses the kidney and the internal thermostat mechanisms of the body. It also stimulates a pain reliever. If young people dance without rest in these hot atmospheres and do not drink a pint of water an hour they can overheat rapidly.
3. The combination of entrance charges , taxis and drug cocktails can cost the raver between £150 - £200 a night.

This is especially worrying for gay men whom often come to club-land looking for an identity and a way to fit in to a community.[4] Yet the majority of the gay clubs demand a simple stern masculinity and body building; a pumping techno intensifies the atmosphere. Ecstasy use becomes almost de rigueur; a requisite accessory to being a proper gay, or, in a wider sense, to being young. In this environment 'E' is often taken by the mouthful just to allow the clubber to feel adequate.

A mass anti-depressant is thus commodified and happiness becomes a thing you buy. When this marketised drug world fails to bring contentment the come-down can be severe. Work, an already surreal activity, can become a drug weary nightmare. Something to get through before you can once more get your happy yet paranoid fix on the weekend.

In these clubs a monopolised black economy thus meets the market economy. It is a world of supply and demand motivated by a repetitive desire to consume and be happy. A perfect combined model of monetarist economics and chemical therapy. Here, Ecstasy use becomes less a tool of insight and more a prop to sustain an unhappy identity and an unhappy culture.

Ode to lost joy

There is a poetic injustice in the way that our society has reacted to the drug culture. Denying any responsibility for creating the need for some mass anti-depressive kick, conservative media and politicians have inadvertently incorporated that need into a weekly market cycle of consumption. 'E' culture is not a passing fad. It is now integral to British culture. The chemical correlative to an inhuman way of life.

Our society is reaching crisis point. It seems we can only function with the use of anti-depressants. 'E' is illegal and its long term psychological and physical effects remain unknown. It has also caused death. Yet similar drugs, such as Prozac, are legal, although equally unquantifiable in terms of long-term effect. They only differ from ecstasy in that they have been researched and medically sanctioned. Within this contradiction, Prozac is ecstasy for the more conventionally minded, and GP's are legalised drug dealers.

At some point the fact that the very basis of social organisation in our society

---

4. *Gay Times* recently conducted a survey that suggested around 48% of 25- 40 year old gay men had taken E.

produces mental instability will have to be faced. Otherwise we will become a nation of addicts with all the social problems that embraces. Politicians owe it to us to replace drugs with a talking cure. What do the British want from their lives? How can work and the economy fulfil those wishes without relying on a deep seated acceptance of misery for its success? They cannot afford to deny us any longer.

There is a common phrase on the rave scene, that "'E' isn't as good as it used to be". Yet many young people are just waiting for the next new drug to come along to see them through their thirties.

THE UNHAPPY SOCIETY: A PEOPLES HISTORY
CHAPTER 10
WHAT'S LEFT FOR THE LEFT?

Throughout much of the twentieth century, the political left proclaimed its own humanistic fantasy of social relations. Theirs was a communal vision known as socialism and they believed in creating a happier society. At the crux of their ideology lay a critique of the free monetarist market, rightly despised as an alienating structure.

In practice Labour executives failed to tackle the power base of the capitalist deputies and were constantly in thrall to the managers of London City and the rentier classes who ruled that important empire. But their vision, their dream, was constant nevertheless.

Their ideals could not have existed without the reality of the market; they were its brave complement, offering people a way out of the misery it produced. But towards the end of the century the British left , fearing that they were unelectable, accepted the fantasy of the right and doffed their caps to the spurious realism of business and social relations built upon monetarist economics. Consequently their rhetoric of a new age became trapped in a capitalist narrative. The country would achieve more in the future; but only economically. Accepting the market in its totality meant that Labour could no longer offer the dawn of a new world. All they had left was small talk of softening capitalism's more abrasive edges.

Tony Blair, the then primate of 'New Labour' put forward a rounded concept of the economic actor. Employees and employers in this model did not act rationally towards the market as the monetarists had suggested, but acted emotively. They worked best with people they trusted in an environment that offered stability. He suggested that work should be consequently structured more communally and less antagonistically. This was an important development that offered hope of building a successful economy that would help people at work achieve contentment by feeling more in power of their own souls . To enshrine this new age of economic relations he developed the policy known as stakeholding.

In one high profile public relations company of the time an administration job provided a central London salary of £6000 per year. A graduate entrance job, £12,000. Employees had to work from 9 am to 10 pm regularly, without overtime pay. To keep them happy the deputies regularly awarded prizes and held parties. A true stakeholding business. Then the next day employees had to work in the same conditions. The pleased smiles on their faces quickly replaced with stressful grimaces. Not surprisingly, these young professionals were major players in the drug culture of the time.

Stakeholding was a realist dream, a way of making work appear worthwhile. But because it was a dream played out over unchanged working conditions its duplicity was felt harder than perhaps the failure of former Labour governments to achieve the socialist utopia. It became just one more corporate strategy to increase productivity for productivity's sake.

Because the 'New Labour' government were fearful of challenging the very basis of business and economic organisation they only tinkered at the edges of social breakdown. The mass riots in London, Manchester, Birmingham and Glasgow following the anarchist crack cocaine parties of the year 2010 were a fitting epitaph to this final failure of the left.

Some years later, at the start of the New Middle Ages, stories were told of the time when money was seen as more important than human happiness. Tales of the terrible time of the unhappy society began to spread across the disparate old city settlements that were then strewn across the country, and people looked back with disgust to the failure of men and women of power to have the courage to change the way of the world.

In the Year of Our Soul 3010

Not such tolerant times

Bilkis Malek

*Amidst the political adulation of 'Asian traits', and
claims to an 'inclusive' national identity, Britain
remains intolerant of South Asian youth.*

Top of the charts

In January 1996 Babylon Zoo with their single *Spaceman* provided the first South
Asian musicians to top the charts. Ten months later Bally Sagoo's single *Dil Cheez*
became the first ever song with full Hindi lyrics to enter the top 20. This year,
Jyoti Mishra, alias White Town, marked the first anniversary of Babylon Zoo's chart
topping single with his own number 1 hit *Your Woman*. Success for Britain's South
Asians has not been confined to the popular music scene, or so we are informed.
Over the last couple of years the British media has painted a (reductive but
sustained) picture of a third generation of South Asians enjoying an increasing
amount of success in areas where majority white youth appear (so it is claimed) to
be faltering. In education South Asian youth have been reported to be more likely
than their white counterparts to stay on in full time education as well as to secure
disproportionately more entry places on degree and HND courses.[1] A few rags to
riches tales, such as self made millionaires Shami Ahmed, owner of Joe Bloggs
Clothing, and Reuben Singh, owner of the fashion accessory chain Miss Attitude,
have been taken as indications that South Asians continue to capitalise on their

---

1. A survey quoted in the programme titled *Relative Values* (24 April 1996, BBC 2)
   indicated that 79 per cent of all South Asians aged 16 - 19 years remained in full time
   education compared to 57 per cent of whites. In addition although South Asians only
   constitute 2.7 per cent of the population, they occupied 6 per cent of all degree and
   HND places.

entrepreneurial traits and flourish in the business sector. And, of course, South Asians have always topped the league for strong family values and loyalty to the community, which have been singled out as the secret behind their currently revered educational and entrepreneurial status.

This image, of an economically successful entrepreneur with virtually impermeable family ties, has coexisted alongside another construction, that of a disaffected South Asian youth unable to come to terms with living in the West. This latter configuration, which has manifested itself in a crusade to document and exaggerate a rise in violence and 'fundamentalist' activity amongst South Asian youth, first emerged in the early 1980s following the 'riots' in Southall and Bradford. It has been given a much more forceful prominence following media coverage of the protests against *The Satanic Verses* and the more recent conflict between police and South Asian youth in Bradford during June 1995. These two almost mythical (and contradictory) constructions have come to dominate debates and commentaries on the experiences of the current generation of young South Asians living in Britain. Whilst neither is able to capture the complexity of what it means to be young, South Asian and living in Britain, politicians and commentators alike continue to manoeuvre between the two. Their simultaneous deployment unveils how Britain has managed to lay claim to a national identity built on 'tolerance' and 'inclusion' without ever shedding its feelings of racial superiority.

John Major's race card with a twist

Politicians on the left began 1997 by renewing their calls for an early general election. Behind the scenes political commentators and critics of the right stepped up their speculation as to when the Tories would play the 'race card'. Meanwhile, John Major was busy packing his suitcase and boarding a plane for a tour of India, Pakistan and Bangladesh. No sooner had he stepped off the plane on his return from the subcontinent than he was on his way to the Commonwealth Institute to mark the 50th anniversary of the independence of India and Pakistan. His keynote address was tailored to flatter and exaggerate similarities between the Conservative party and a section of the voting population highly concentrated in marginal seats. Reiterating his favoured public colloquy during the subcontinent tour, the prime minister praised the majority South Asian audience for their contribution to British society, describing their entrepreneurial skills, commitment to self help and strong family values as 'instinctively Conservative'.

A central theme in Major's speech was to depict Britain as a multicultural society characterised by a mood of 'tolerance' for individuals of different races and backgrounds. He painted a picture of race relations in Britain as being free of the racial tension predicted by earlier politicians and commentators who 'feared a trench war between light and dark skinned people' (a reference to Enoch Powell and Margaret Thatcher). Whilst he made a clear attempt to acknowledge that black people in Britain continue to be disadvantaged in comparison with their white counterparts, this was placed within the context of an unfinished job which, when complete, would 'make Britain the best place to live'. The hand-picked onlookers, predominantly Conservative supporters, responded with a standing ovation, whilst the premier himself was decorated with a garland. An altogether pristine performance but one which is unlikely to have touched the hearts and everyday experiences of large sections of the South Asian population in Britain.

Major's 'tolerant Britain' is unlikely to have rung true for the young South Asians residing in the Manningham area of Bradford (the focus of media attention following conflict with police in June 1995); nor with Mukhtar Ahmed (permanently disfigured following an attack by a group of white youths in the East End of London), Richard Everitt (murdered near the Kings Cross area of North London by a group of young South Asians in August 1994), and the many others who have suffered the worst consequences of racial tension, prejudice and violence. In addition, the image of the successful Asian entrepreneur remains far removed from the everyday realities of the vast majority of South Asian youth, in particular those of Pakistani and Bangladeshi background who (along with those of African Caribbean descent) experience higher rates of unemployment than any other ethnic group.[2]

For many young South Asians, perhaps as frustrating as John Major's reductive construction of a British South Asian experience topping the charts in education, employment and family values, is the absence of any effective alternative from the other two leading parties. Unable to offer a constructive challenge to John Major's words, Labour and Liberal Democrat representatives (the most publicised responses coming from Keith Vaz and Paddy Ashdown

---

2. Figures for Spring 1995, collated by the Labour Force Survey, indicate that the unemployment rates across Great Britain for the 16-24 age group were 39 per cent for the two categories 'Pakistani/Bangladeshi' and 'Black'; 23 per cent for 'Indian' and 14 per cent for 'White'.

respectively) resorted to pointing out the hypocrisy of the prime minister whose party has always been harsh on immigration. Indeed those still eagerly awaiting the conventional Tory 'race card' in order to display their antiracist sensibilities would have been well advised to take the opportunity to revise their understanding of British racism.[3] For this was John Major's race card, only in a language more associated with the left.

Despite popular perceptions of the Conservative Party as being less concerned for the well being of ethnic minorities, the current perceptions and attitudes towards the South Asian electorate are virtually identical amongst the leading political contenders. This was made apparent in May 1996 when the leaders of the three main political parties were invited to participate in a programme broadcast as part of the BBC series *East*.[4] The interviewer, Martin Bashir, asked each politician to outline why members of the Asian population should vote for their respective party at the next general election.

John Major sought to identify similarities between 'Asian traits' and Conservative Party policies. In a similar vein, Tony Blair attempted to reveal the appeal of his party to the Asian electorate by claiming a mutual 'ethos and morality'. New Labour's vision of 'a society of ambition and aspiration matched by compassion, decency and support for strong local communities and individuals' was, stated Tony Blair, 'a language very much that Asian people would understand'. Paddy Ashdown began his contribution by stating that the Asian electorate would benefit in three ways from a Liberal Democrat government which would 'provide opportunity', 'a share in power' and 'fight discrimination'. As the interview proceeded it became clear that Ashdown's understanding of the dynamics characterising the everyday lives of the British Asian population was informed by the same stereotypes embedded in the opening statements of his two contemporaries. When he was asked to explain how his party proposed to reduce the increase in Asian juvenile crime he responded that it would be curbed in the same way as juvenile crime committed by any other group. He added, 'it must be of great worry to the Asian community, a community so far best known in Britain for its stability, its family values and law abiding nature

---

3. See for example John Sweeney's article 'Major Rises Above Mockery In Bid To Become Man of All Races', *The Observer*, 19 January 1997. Also see leader comment on p23 in the same issue.
4. The programme entitled *A Power in the land* was broadcast on 29 May 1996.

being suddenly infected by the same things others are'.

Implicit in each party leader's response was a pathological view of Asians in general and Asian family life in particular. In this instance, the stereotypes of a natural flair for business, close knit family, strong traditions and moral values - successfully used by Thatcher and Enoch Powell to highlight an 'alien' presence in Britain and thereby legitimise stricter immigration controls - were being manoeuvred to win 'Asian votes'. However, it would be wrong to assume that in the 1990s British politics and politicians have moved beyond a concern to control/restrict the presence of black people in this country. The Asylum and Immigration Bill introduced towards the end of 1995 is but one indication that the 'British' are far from overcoming their 'fear of being swamped by people with a different culture'.[5] In addition, a closer examination of the current trend amongst political leaders of promoting 'Asian values and customs' (once seen as incompatible with a British national identity) as desirable national traits reveals how Britain's politicians have, as Kenan Malik has suggested, appropriated 'antiracist themes for chauvinist ends'.[6]

Behind the lingo of multiculturalism and antiracism

The current generation of South Asian youth have grown up in a period where it is increasingly commonplace to hear of Britain's good record on race relations, better than any other in Europe. Such affirmations are largely due to the fact that multiculturalism and antiracism (and their various initiatives) have become very much a part of the national vocabulary. From the national curriculum to the police force, from equal opportunity policies to ethnic monitoring, never before has Britain as a nation been so keen to project its tolerance of different cultures and races. Yet this national drive to promote a multicultural Britain has not resulted in a reduction in racism. Antiracist and/or multicultural initiatives have certainly provided the opportunity for well meaning people to declare, with much more regularity, zero tolerance for racial harassment and discrimination, and to abhor the activities of extreme right groups such

5. The Asylum and Immigration Bill introduced a 'white list' to indicate countries (including Pakistan, India, Sri Lanka and Nigeria) from where applications for asylum may still be assessed, but would in the first instance be accepted as being from 'safe' countries and therefore likely to be bogus. Claude Moraes, director of the Joint Council for the Welfare of Immigrants, has highlighted how the new Bill 'has blurred the distinction between asylum and immigration and successfully linked both with fraud and illegality'. (Moraes, 1995, p6).
6. Kenan Malik, *The Meaning of Race*, Macmillan, London 1996.

as the BNP and Combat 18. However, they have done little to dislodge the feelings of racial superiority that continue to pervade Britain and the west.

What some have called the 'new racism' has undergone a transition in 1980s and 1990s Britain, taking on an increasingly more insidious character. And this transition is captured in the way in which Major and his two leading rivals have distanced themselves from Thatcher and Powell in their appropriation of Asian 'traits'. Whilst an essentialist notion of 'Asian' has remained very much intact in the run up to the 1997 general election, what has been modified is the way in which 'Asian traits' are currently being appropriated in relation to a British national identity. Once deemed a threat to the 'British way of life', 'Asian traits' have suddenly become the envy of the nation. A key question this raises is, 'Why at this particular political conjuncture has there been such a shift in attitudes towards 'Asian traits'?' Part of the answer lies in Kenan Malik's recent assertion that 'tolerance', 'antiracism' and 'multiculturalism' have become convenient themes utilised by the state to re-assert a superior (in that it can lay claim to having the best record on race relations) cohesive national identity (in that the nation is united in the fight against racism). Thus, at a time when politicians have become fixed on the 'breakdown of family values' as a major factor in the increase in juvenile crime, drug abuse, and the rise in the number of young single mothers, etc., it is not surprising that they have found it beneficial to use the South Asian population, with its 'track record on strong family values', in their respective visions of a future Britain.

By speaking of 'Asian traits' as being in synch with 'a British way of life' politicians may well believe that they can lay claim to promoting a tolerant, inclusive, multicultural society. Two observations suggest that this equation isn't as simple as it is made to appear. Firstly, it is only because so called 'Asian traits' happen to 'chime' in with current political priorities and ideas on the basis for a unified national identity that the notion 'British' is being promoted as being 'inclusive' of 'Asian values and customs'. Britishness has not been revised specifically to include Asians. Rather it is the degree to which Asians are able to display characteristics defined as 'British', that their inclusion within a national identity is endorsed.[7] Secondly, the reductive

---

7. This is further supported by the fact that, despite invitations by the organisation Operation Black Vote, the leading politicians have not made themselves visible amongst the African Caribbean population. Perhaps, given their current priorities of strong family ties and economic growth, it has not been so easy to accommodate their understanding of 'African Caribbean traits' within their vision of Britain.

construction of 'Asian' interwoven into each party leader's attempt to obtain the support of the Asian electorate has never captured the complex and diverse experiences of British South Asians. Behaviour amongst people of South Asian descent deemed inconsistent with 'Asian traits' (as in Paddy Ashdown's response to Asian juvenile crime), is explained in terms of a 'clash of cultures' - one culture 'infecting' another. Thus, alongside claims of Britain's tolerant character and good record on race relations, there are intermittent reminders of the dangers/ incompatibility of different cultures living side by side. In other words, if at this moment in British history 'Asian traits' are being mobilised by politicians to convey an inclusive image of Britain, then events such as the Bradford 'riots' have provided the same politicians with an opportunity to re-emphasise and maintain an exclusive national identity.

The persistence in locating and understanding public protests by South Asian youth and their confrontations with state authorities in the context of 'culture clash' disregards the extent to which British racism has been central to the anger currently being expressed. This is not to say that all, or even the vast majority of, South Asian youth have reacted to British racism in the same way. However, I do believe that the protests which have captured the attention of the British media reveal the intensity of what I can only describe as a 'cumulative' tension and frustration, which has arisen from an insidious form of British racism and not from the activities of the BNP or any other far right group. What the state and Britain as a whole has failed to realise is that incidents such as the 'street violence' in Manningham can no more be interpreted as a clash of cultures or intergenerational conflict than the public burning of *The Satanic Verses* can be attributed to fundamentalist activity. Writing about the 'Rushdie affair', Tariq Modood makes an important point about reports linking the reaction of Bradford's young Muslims to fundamentalism:[8]

I doubt that there are more than a few thousand fundamentalists in Britain and most of them are likely to be in London rather than Bradford, in offices

8. In the context of this essay it is important to note that although Islam is not the religion of all British South Asians, as Avtar Brah points out: 'Racism against South Asians in ... the late twentieth century ... represents a reconstitution of "the Asian" ... through a foregrounding of "the Muslim"' (p169 in *Cartographies of Diaspora*, Routledge, London 1996).

rather than factories. Asian fundamentalists are urban, educated and middle-class: British Asian Muslims have rural peasant origins.[9]

The source of the deep seated anger clearly present in the 'Rushdie affair' is to be found in the subtle messages of racial superiority embedded in the everyday language of antiracism and multiculturalism. And it is not specific to Bradford's young Muslims. It is equally present in the Kings Cross area of North London, where Richard Everitt was murdered, as it perhaps was when four Asian youths recently paraded Pakistan's national flag from their car on Eid, near my parents' home in the North West of England.[10] This anger is 'cumulative' in that its origins cannot be reduced to one single event or moment: it has gained gradual intensity from the unchanging claims to racial superiority that the west continues to assert over the rest of the world. The subtle messages of racial superiority/inferiority occur almost daily, but are not so easily exposed and challenged precisely because they are submerged within an emphasis on equality and tolerance. John Major's speech at the Commonwealth Institute serves as a good example. His repeated emphasis on the 'inclusive' 'tolerant' character of the British was interspersed with comments such as 'if you share our love of country'. This token and reductive inclusion of South Asians in a British national identity can also be detected in Dale Winton's comment, 'I bet you've never heard of him', in his introduction to Bally Sagoo on the *National Lottery* programme.[11] Both these instances illustrate the everyday reminders of a marginal and inferior national status granted to British South Asians and black people in general by self proclaimed antiracists. In John Major's case, if Britain really was a nation 'inclusive' of its multicultural multiracial population would it really be necessary to speak in terms such as 'you' and 'our'. As for the climax of Dale Winton's introduction of Bally Sagoo, the fact that most viewers tuning into the *National Lottery* programme may not have heard of this artist is not the issue. The subtext in Dale Winton's introduction is exposed when placed in the context that national identity is often measured with regards to an individual's

9. T. Madood, *Race, Culture Difference*, James Donald and Ali Rattansi (eds), Sage, London 1992, p266.
10. The body language of many onlookers suggested that they were infuriated by this act. Clearly a very different response from the one drawn by the parading of the Union Jack during events such as VE day and England's World Cup victory against Holland during Euro '96.
11. Broadcast on 11 January 1997 on BBC1

ability to recount certain events, symbols, icons, personalities, which have been accorded 'official' national status. Thus, whilst unfamiliarity with Bally Sagoo is unlikely to taint an individuals claim to being 'British', the opposite is most likely to be the case as regards personalities such as Bobby Moore and William Shakespeare.

British politicians, of whichever political inclination, have through the language of multiculturalism and antiracism, maintained a silence on issues of race and racism. This has also been a weakness in current debates/theorisations amongst the academic left in regard to the dynamics characterising the cultural politics of black British youth. In making such an assertion I am not claiming that the racism of the state has escaped the attention of the academic left. Indeed it has been precisely within these circles that the limitations of multicultural and antiracist initiatives have been exposed . However, issues of race and racism have largely remained absent from the exploration and appropriation of notions such as hybridity and diaspora which have become central to current academic debates about black British identities.

Race and racism in the cultural politics of British South Asian youth

The detailed and sometimes complex investigations into notions of hybridity and diaspora have drawn attention to the cross cultural 'fusions' / 'creolisation' of distinct cultural forms that characterise the experiences of populations with a migratory background.[12] This work has been at the forefront of exposing the fallibility of monolithic concepts of culture and cultural location. Whilst its contribution to claiming a space for black people within more flexible notions of Britishness and Englishness cannot be underestimated, two observations lead me to question the centrality of the idea of cross cultural 'fusions', and hence its ability fully to appreciate the dynamics characterising the cultural politics of British South Asian youth.

The first observation is that, whilst reports claiming a rise in violence or fundamentalist activity amongst South Asian youth must be challenged for their assertions that such behaviour is widespread, and questioned for the reductive explanations they often afford, they are not to be dismissed lightly. The mood of anger conveyed in these reports might be articulated in a variety of different ways, but it is an emotion felt by an increasing number of young South Asians.

---

12. I don't have the space here to describe this work in any detail but for a summary of contemporary appropriations of hybridity and diaspora see Robert Young's chapter, 'Hybridity and Diaspora' in his book *Colonial Desire*, Routledge, London 1995.

The recurrent subtle messages of racial superiority/inferiority, from which this anger arises, are significant in the negotiation of cultural locations amongst diaspora and hybrid populations. They increasingly draw the individual to question the feasibility/desirability of consolidating the multiple cultural influences and experiences of being South Asian and living in Britain. Sallie Westwood's discussion of the comments afforded by the interviewees in a study of black and Asian people diagnosed as schizophrenic touches on the point I am trying to make.[13] Many of the biographical accounts collated in the study highlighted 'the deep ambivalence that surrounds blackness' as conveyed in the statement from one of the female interviewees 'I don't enjoy being a black woman. Given the chance I would change that'. Within my own wider family network I have witnessed a handful of individuals of my generation (by no means the vast majority) who in their teens were keen to participate in a wide range of social and cultural experiences, and maintain a pluralist outlook, but who now, in their mid to late 20s, find solace in groups like the Hizb ut Tahrir which openly asserts anti-Semitic, anti-Western and homophobic attitudes. Whilst the vast majority continue to negotiate identities which provide a sense of belonging without resorting to the ideas of ethnic absolutism it cannot be denied that being South Asian and British is not something that is as easily consolidated as the current appropriations of diaspora and hybridity have tended to suggest.

The second observation I'd like to make is that the cross-cultural locations negotiated by migrant populations are not void of the racial and cultural hierarchies constructed by western racisms. My own attention has been drawn to this in the context of an exploratory study on the use of films on videotape amongst British South Asian audiences. Statistics from a questionnaire survey revealed that, far from a decline in the consumption of cinematic products from their parents'/grandparents' country of origin, the film culture of British South Asian youth is generally inclusive of popular films from both the west and the Indian subcontinent. This would seem to lend weight to the dialogic identities asserted by the notions of hybridity and diaspora, in that the film culture of the majority of respondents aged 16-24 consisted of two distinct categories of film which deploy very different cinematic, linguistic and cultural codes.[14]

13. Sallie Westwood, 'Racism, Mental Illness and the Politics of Identity' in *Racism, Modernity and Identity*, Ali Rattansi and Sallie Westwood (eds), Polity Press, Cambridge 1994.

However, in pilot discussions and informal conversations during the distribution of the questionnaire, it became apparent that the aesthetic qualities of both categories of film tended to be measured according dominant western aesthetics. As one 23-year-old female stated, 'Storyline keeps you going in English films because it's very strong. The way it's directed the way it's made and presented, it's really interesting, imagination is used. In Indian films, storylines it's all the same, it's rubbish. The only reason I watch it is because of the songs'.

These findings are similar to Marie Gillespie's study of the consumption and reception of various media texts amongst South Asian youth in Southall.[15] Gillespie's research suggested that whilst the majority of the sample were 'just as likely to have seen recent blockbusters from Hollywood as those from Bombay' there was also evidence of 'a fierce rejection of Hindi films as a "genre", especially among boys' whose criticisms echoed 'western critical discourses'. Without an adequate exploration of the power relations which give rise to such dynamics in consumption, there is a danger of presenting migrant populations in the west as cultural dopes always prone to assimilation into western culture. This is precisely the trap into which Gillespie falls, as can be seen in her assertion that 'these may be "diaspora kids" but their aspirations for travel and lifestyle are essentially American'. However, the similarities between the two studies with regard to trends in consumption and critical evaluation of popular/mainstream and Indian films does alert attention to the presence of racial and cultural hierarchies (constructed by dominant western discourses), not only in the interstices in which diaspora and hybrid identities are contested, but also within cross cultural expressions and subject positionings.

In light of the above observations I am not so sure that the current generation of black British youth is as comfortable as Stuart Hall recently suggested, in just 'going on being black and being British'.[16] These observations are not necessarily new; in recent years other writers have also drawn attention to similar issues. Paul Gilroy has asserted that the difficulty with ... 'the cultural saturnalia which attends the end of the innocent black subject ... is that in leaving racial essentialism behind by viewing "race" itself as a social and cultural construction, it has been insufficiently

---

14. Of the 16-24 age group popular / mainstream films were watched by 83.5 per cent compared to 81 per cent for Indian films.
15. See Marie Gillespie's book, *Television, Ethnicity and Cultural Change*, Routledge, London 1995.

alive to the lingering power of specifically racialised forms of power and subordination'.[17] Avtar Brah's exploration of 'the multiple configurations of power' present in the negotiation and construction of diaspora locations is also pertinent to the points I am trying to raise here.

I have not presented my observations in any complete form to be neatly slotted into relevant academic work. Rather they are offered as points which I feel should be debated much more at the centre of discussions about diaspora and hybrid experiences, and not outside or on the margins, as has often been the case to date. Without such a shift, work in this area remains limited in any contribution it might make towards putting race and racism back onto the mainstream political agenda.

Conclusion

The 'trench warfare' might not have exploded on a scale sufficient to disturb John Major's view of Britain as a 'tolerant' nation, but it continues to affect the everyday lives of British South Asian youth. As individuals, the three leading politicians may well believe they are fully committed to the sustaining of an 'inclusive' Britain, but this is unlikely to be realised through being seen in temples or photographed donning garland(s) at key events in the South Asian communities (in recent months Blair and Major have been particularly prone to this). Paddy Ashdown can be as passionate as he likes about standing up for the victims of racial harassment in his local constituency, but if he were to be in power he is unlikely to progress very far in eradicating racism when his own party is unable to shed its racist members.[18]

As I write, it remains to be seen if John Major is to have the last laugh in the 1997 general election or whether he is to be displaced at Number 10 by Tony Blair and his entourage. However, if there is to be a truly inclusive place for South Asian youth in British society, then the next government, of whichever political affiliation, would do well to begin by conceding that British racism is testing the tolerance of this section of the population.

---

16. Stuart Hall's keynote address at the 'Frontlines Backyards' conference held at the Institute of Education on 6 December 1996. However, in quoting Hall's comment, which was with particular reference to the Afro Caribbean experience, I do not wish to homogenise diaspora and hybrid experiences (these will vary between as well as within different groups).
17. From p.32 in Gilroy, P. *The Black Atlantic*, Verso, 1993.
18. In the 1993 local elections in Tower Hamlets some Liberal Democrats were accused of resorting to racist leafleting in order to secure the majority white vote in the Isle of Dogs.

University *of* East London

Department of Cultural Studies

The Department was awarded a '5' rating in the 1996 HEFCE research assessment exercise and an 'excellent' in the teaching quality assessment. It is now offering three innovative taught MAs:

MA Cultural Studies

Topics covered include: History & Psychoanalysis; Modernity & Twentieth Century Consumption; New Media; Popular Music; Postcolonial Theory & Cultural Forms.

MA Women's Studies

Topics covered include: Cyberfeminism; Feminist Theory & Visual Culture; Queer Theory & Representation; Feminism and the Women's Movement; Black Feminism.

MA Refugee Studies

Topics covered include: Introduction to Forced Migration; Refugee Law; Refugee Communities and Social Policy; Cultures of Exile; project on refugee communities in Britain.

All programmes include foundation, research and dissertation units. Students may select options from all three programmes. Some fee bursaries are available.

The Department also offers PhD research supervision in a wide range of areas.

For further information about any of the courses shown above, contact Frances Wells, tel: 0181 849 3545, email: wells3@uel.ac.uk.

UNIVERSITY *of* EAST LONDON UeL

Reading identity
Young Black British men

Elaine Pennicott

Fiction by young black writers is one place where different stories can be told.

We are shut out of so many areas, like TV, which is such a powerful medium, so that our stories are told for us ... With books it's a lot easier, especially if you have got companies like X Press. We have got so many stories that haven't been told and the books are a way of communicating ... even if I can't be there to take part in the conversations, I feel I am able to communicate.

Yana Richardson, interview, 16.08.96

The idea that there exists a knowable 'black youth' seems obvious. Leading figures across the political spectrum - Police Commissioner Sir Paul Condon, Labour MP Kate Hoey, radical black organisations such as Panther - all claim an intimate knowledge of the truth about 'black youth': mugger of old ladies, rioter, illegal immigrant, drug dealer, athlete, problem of the inner cities, rebel, soul brother, funkateer. The otherness of black masculinity has been narrated through these apocryphal myths. It has been perceived as a problem, something which is at odds with, and on the margins of, British society, and which cannot be incorporated into definitions of Britishness. Black men have been labelled, discussed and viewed as a problem that needs sorting out.

Party politics at the end of the 1990s continues to indulge in these myths. New Labour's successful attempt to occupy the middle ground of British politics has reinforced the marginalisation of groups which do not occupy 'Middle England'. The 'conservative modernity' proposed by Blair with its reassertion of family and social values relies upon an image - similar to that of Enoch Powell or Margaret Thatcher - of the violent inner city inhabited by hostile outsiders, in particular unemployable black youth: sexually irresponsible, potentially violent, and demanding valuable resources from an embattled state sector.

I am particularly interested in how young people of colour respond to these myths, which have dominated public spaces of representation for so long, and which constantly demonise and marginalise them. For the stories they tell about themselves are more interesting and revealing than the stories that are told about them. The mainstream and the political parties, with their narrow understanding of what it is to be British, do not see the many ways in which young black men engage in everyday, ordinary British life. Their lives have been ignored except when they coincide with dominant myths of 'Black Youth'. Then they become examples of 'we told you so', for that is 'obviously' and 'naturally' what they are like.

There is now a popular fiction written by young black people which represents a fertile and popular place of aesthetic and political expression. This literature clearly demonstrates the desires, pleasures and pain of living in modern British society, and how young Britons of colour are refusing to engage in any simplistic way with the dominant images and myths about themselves. The persistent narratives of 'Black youth' are considered, are tried on for size, are played with, rather than simply adopted or rejected. The emergence of a Black British popular literature demonstrates the extent to which young Black people take part actively, albeit less formally and less visibly, in British cultural and political life.

Popular fiction, like music, photography and film, is a symbolic place where myths of and about black youth can be reenacted, challenged and reconstituted. In the 1990s it has become an important element in this performance. It provides a site which is more or less outside the control of the dominant forms of fiction and publishing, where young Black Britons can more freely tell their stories, express their creativity and set up conversations with others. This article is partly based on interviews with two people involved in black publishing and writing - Diran Adebayo, winner of the 1996 Saga prize for literature with his novel *Some Kind of Black* (Virago 1996), and Doton Adebayo, who, with Steve Pope, set up the publishers X Press.

The Yardie myth

X Press began producing popular literature written by black authors for black audiences in the late 1980s. Their books were an immediate success, particularly *Yardie* by Victor Headley, which has since become a trilogy. *Yardie* is an old fashioned and rather moralistic gangsta tale, set not in the streets of New York, but around Brixton, Hackney and Finsbury Park. It tells of illegal immigrants, drug dealing and gang warfare. Targeted specifically at young, metropolitan black people, it was initially sold outside clubs and dance halls and in local newsagents. The success of *Yardie*, and Augustus Patrick's *Baby Father*, resulted in the sale of film rights to the BBC, the sale of publishing rights to Pan Books, and the expansion of X Press's catalogue to include young unknown black British authors. Subsequently, large book shops, such as WH Smiths, created specific sections for black literature. Dotun Adebayo says of this time,

> Within something like 9 months we sold 12,000 copies, of which maybe half was through bookstalls and the other half was through non-book outlets, whether it was us directly selling them or via a Pattie shop, or a hairdresser's or a record store or whatever ... now we take for granted that when we go to W H Smiths, or at least to a W H Smiths in a black area, we are going to see a stand for black interest books (interview 16.8.96).

Yardie quickly entered in to the wider popular imagination. *The Independent*, *Daily Mail* and *Observer* all carried features on Headley and the 'Yardie drug culture', with headlines such as 'Yardie's Evil' and 'New racism finds a Yardie stick'. The novel was seen as an index of the black population in general, and black men in particular. Headley was reviewed as simply telling the truth about black life in London. The *Hackney Gazette* wrote: 'he admits the authentic detail of the novel comes from an intimate knowledge of the secret wheeling and dealing of the gangsters ... totally accurate representation of the Yardie drugs scene in Hackney' (29.6.92).

    Yardie was reviewed as being 'so real' that Headley had to leave the country after it was published, in fear of retribution from those in London who thought he 'knew too much'. It is also reputedly recommended reading at the police training school in Hendon. Whether this is myth or fact, it indicates the extent to which *Yardie* entered the public realm of fantasy and myth about Black men and inner city life.

Yardie came to exemplify 'black youth' as a vilified version of young masculinity. The right wing media condemned Headley and X Press for advocating violence and drug dealing. But black organisations also condemned them for reproducing negative, racist images of the black community. Doton comments on this tension:

> There are stereotypes within our community, but I don't know anybody who is in the business to produce them, that would be suicidal, unless you are saying that our readership is so stupid that they can't see through stereotypes. They see them every day. The same people that write the books are reading the books. They are ordinary people, they choose the topics to write about, they write about them from black perspectives.

For Doton, stories are a crucial way in which Black Britons can give form to the contradictory and often painful experience of living in modern Britain, and he dismisses the attempts to reduce the different concerns and expressions of identity to a one dimensional image. Literature is an essentially political practice. Young black men, he asserts, are engaged in complex negotiations with other black men, with women, with white people, as well as with the myth of Black Youth - negotiations that are taking place on many different sites.

The myths that circulated about *Yardie* delimited the space of cultural imagination which framed the knowledge of young black men. The response to the book revealed more about popular perceptions of black masculinity than it did about the lives of young black men. Writing about colonised subjects in France in the 1950s and 1960s, Frantz Fanon, in *Black Skin White Masks*, noted that in the colonial imagination the Negro was less a person and more a public site on which different fantasies and fears were played out. The Negro, he argued, didn't really exist outside of the stereotypes that circulated knowledge about him to the general French population. The myth of 'black youth' today functions in a similar way. It tells more truths about the fears and fascinations of our society than it does of young people of colour living in Britain. Myth operates as a sort of public space - a territory of representation that is at times remarkably familiar but at others quite alien, yet distinctly and uniquely British. The myth of 'black youth' has very little to do with individual young black men. It is a place they visit, along with the rest of the British population, but one they are forced to occupy when the dominant white gaze is upon them.

Black flaneurs

'Black youth' is articulated in the framework of a rhetoric, and fear, of Americanisation: images of hoods, crack-dealers and street killings. British black youth is defined in relationship to this dystopia of the American inner city. The work of French poet Charles Pierre Baudelaire (1821-1867) proves useful for prizing free young black British men from this stereotypical habitat. Baudelaire evoked a mythical Paris, one which celebrated the dislocation and the unsettling experiences of modernity. The natural inhabitant of this modern city was the flaneur who, picking his way through the streets and spaces of the city, learnt to master it. 'Black youth' can be reinterpreted as modern day flaneurs or dandies, who live outside the anachronistic fantasy called middle England, in a place that is always constructed as Other to the respectable. Baudelaire's vision of the city, with its sense of decay, from which lives and loves can grow, constructs subjects who do not fit easily into the stereotypes of good and bad. Rather they become implicated in the fears and fantasies that attempt to define them.

Victor Headley writes about this modern day flaneur, and maps out his city. His characters D, Piper, and Charlie parade the streets of Hackney and Brixton in their meticulously chosen clothes. They know London, its hidden dance halls and drinking places. The London they inhabit comes to life at night when ordinary citizens are in bed, and the London bobby is replaced by the vice and serious crime squads. D is an outsider, the antithesis of 'middle England'. His codes of behaviour and language can only be understood by those who know and live in the metropolis. He lives on the margins, running gangs and dealing drugs. D in a strange way, represents the working-class hero who, struggling against the violence and prejudice of his society, comes to master it.

Diran Adebayo writes about a different city. But it is still one in which modern flaneurs inhabit the street - that mythical place. *Some Kind of Black* tells the story of Dele, an Oxford student who inhabits a paradoxical world, part of the elite of British society, and part of the Brixton street. Unlike D in *Yardie*, Adebayo's main characters come from Nigeria. He writes in awareness of the myth of 'black youth', yet he refuses to be defined by it. His is a London inhabited not by gangstas but different 'selves' in negotiation and conversation with each other: 'you get a very sharp sense of how identity isn't static at all but is made up of your reactions to the kinds of selves you have to be.'

He writes of a city that is not simply a place where those outside respectable British society live but a London where young men play with different identities and perform their masculinity depending on the social and cultural context; be it a 'little ghetto jive' to attract a pretty, middle-class Oxford student, or acting the 'original gentleman' to a pretty 'home maker rather than butt-shaker'. Adebayo demonstrates how, in the city, young men engage with the dominant myths of black people - which place them in centres such as Brixton, which insist they are Jamaican, that they all came over here in the 1950s, that they are not academic and so on - what he calls the orthodoxy of black life. His writing engages with the complex and ambivalent ways in which young black men negotiate the experience of modern life, of police violence, of the demands of parents who emigrated to England with dreams and hopes but watched as they withered, of childhood friends who choose to conform to the low expectations of them held by British society.

Unlike Headley who is sited in the marginal, mythic Black areas of London, Adebayo is much more unsure of his place in London:

> I find it difficult in terms of where to live in London because I am a member of a lot of different homes. Maybe more homes than most people have in a sense - I'm kind of from Nigeria but I haven't actually been to Nigeria, so I can't have an automatic claim to various Nigerian heartlands like north west London, as other people do ... [also] private school ... obviously black. I feel a bit off centre, it's just kind of difficult to find a place where I can feel that, yes, this is my area.

Adebayo cannot write with certainty about his place in London because like other young black men, he cannot easily fit himself in to the stereotypical images or areas of black masculinity. He is uncomfortable with the orthodoxy of black life, because it forces him to enact a role which is partly alien to him. Whilst he is black, he is not Jamaican; he walks the streets late at night, but he is not selling drugs. The approval of his father is deeply important to him, yet his values are different. But the orthodoxy is still deeply attractive. It provides a way in which black men can communicate through a short-hand of shared experience - on the one hand of excessive social attention, for example from the police, yet on the other the invisibility of everyday, institutional and local racism.

What is clear from the examples of Headley and Adebayo is that young black British men are refusing to engage in any simplistic way with the dominant images and myths about them. Their identities are not fixed by history or biology, but, like all identities, are performed and acted out in relationship to the many different cultural and political contexts they are in. The idea that there is a knowable 'black youth' is constantly challenged by a performativity which questions its mythology. black men going to Oxford University, black men staying at home to look after their children, black men who know and respect their fathers. The urban spaces that these men inhabit may not be recognised by the dominant white British society, but it is a mistake to assume that they therefore do not exist.

Soundings

Soundings is a journal of politics and culture. It is a forum for ideas which aims to explore the problems of the present and the possibilities for a future politics and society. Its intent is to encourage innovation and dialogue in progressive thought. Half of each future issue will be devoted to debating a particular theme: topics in the pipeline include: Africa, Active Welfare in Britain, America, and The European Left.

Why not subscribe?
Make sure of your copy

Subscription rates, 1997 (3 issues)

INDIVIDUAL SUBSCRIPTIONS: UK - £35.00   *Rest of the World - £45.0*
INSTITUTIONAL SUBSCRIPTIONS UK - £70.00   *Rest of the World - £80.00*

Please send me one year's subscription starting with Issue Number _____

I enclose payment of £ _____

I wish to become a supporting subscriber and enclose a donation of £ _____

I enclose total payment of £ _____

Name _____

Address _____

_____

_____ Postcode _____

Please return this form with cheque or money order payable to Soundings and send to:

Soundings, c/o Lawrence & Wishart, 99A Wallis Road, London E9 5LN

Underworked and underpaid

Ian Brinkley

Free market logic says that low pay creates jobs.
Has this worked for young people?

What has happened to youth unemployment and employment is a key test of whether the Government's strategy of labour market deregulation has worked. The under 25s have in many ways born the full brunt of the removal and weakening of employment protections, cuts in welfare benefits, and the decline of trade union organisation and membership. If deregulation works, young people should have done better than the national average in the mid 1990s compared with the mid 1980s.

Are young people doing better or worse than the average?

The evidence shows that, far from doing better than the average, the relative position of the under 25s has worsened in the 1990s. Chart 1 shows ILO unemployment rates from spring 1984 to spring 1996 (1984 is the earliest year for which ILO unemployment rates on a consistent definition are available). Two conclusions can be drawn:

- Firstly, the gap between the unemployment rate for all ages and the unemployment rate for the under 25s seems to be greater in the mid 1990s than in the mid 1980s. In other words, compared to the national average, young people are doing worse.

- Secondly, the differences between youth rates and the national rate narrowed in the 1980s labour market recovery. There has been no narrowing in the unemployment rate in the 1990s recovery.

These conclusions are not significantly affected by the inclusion or exclusion in the figures of young people combining full-time education and work - the idea that the overall picture might be distorted by an increase in the number of students flooding the jobs market in search of part-time work does not seem to be true.

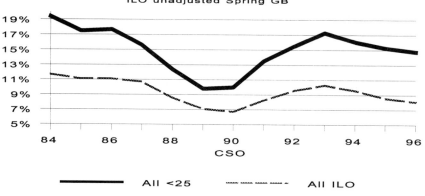

Chart 1: Relative Youth Unemployment Worsens
ILO unadjusted Spring GB

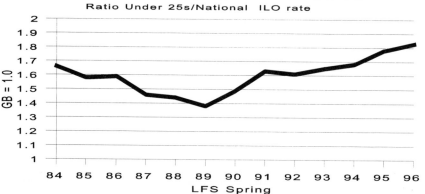

Chart 2: Youth Unemployment Compared
Ratio Under 25s/National ILO rate

The difference between youth and national rates can be more clearly shown as a ratio. For under 25s the unemployment rate in spring 1994 was 19.4 per cent for under 25s against a national average of 11.7 per cent, so that youth unemployment was 1.66 times the national average. In spring 1996 the unemployment rate for under 25s was 14.8 per cent for under 25s against 8.1 per cent for the national average, so that youth unemployment was 1.83 times the national average. This is shown in chart 2 which compares the unemployment rate for under 25s and all ILO unemployed between spring 1984 and spring 1996. This is all the more surprising because, as shown in chart 2, the 1980s recovery saw the differences in unemployment rates for young people and the rest of the workforce become smaller. This simply did not happen in this recovery.

Younger men in particular suffer from very high ILO unemployment rates and their relative position has worsened significantly since 1984. In spring 1984 the unemployment rate for young men under 25 was 1.62 times the national average, but in spring 1996 it was nearly 2.2 times the national average. Younger women had similar unemployment rates to young men in the mid 1980s but have since seen some relative improvement. In spring 1984 the ratio between young women's unemployment rate and the national average was 1.55 times, but by spring 1996 this had fallen to 1.37 times.

The improving position for young women seems largely to reflect the general relative improvement in women's labour market position over the past decade, as measured by ILO unemployment rates. For example, in spring 1984 the average ILO unemployment rate for men was 11.8 per cent and for women 11.5 per cent. By spring 1996 the male average ILO unemployment rate was 9.6 per cent, while the female ILO unemployment rate was 6.3 per cent.

When the unemployment rates for young men are compared with the overall male unemployment rate and the unemployment rates for young women are compared with overall unemployment rates for women, then the difference between the sexes largely disappears (see chart 3). In other words, when young women are compared with the female average unemployment rate, they are doing just as badly, relatively speaking, as when young men are compared with the male average unemployment rate.

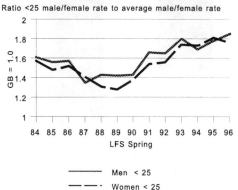

Chart 3: Unemployment Ratio by Sex

Ratio <25 male/female rate to average male/female rate

LFS Spring

——— Men < 25

— — · Women < 25

The worsening position of young people compared with the national average also took place despite a major decline in the numbers of young people competing for work. Between spring 1989 and spring 1996 the total population of under 25s fell from 7.6 million to 6.3 million, a drop of 18 per cent. Over the same period the proportion in full-time education increased from 20 per cent to 35 per cent. The numbers active in the labour market (in work or looking for work, including students) fell from 6.1 million to 4.4 million, a fall of 27 per cent. If those in full-time education are excluded, the fall in the total numbers active was from 5.5 million to 3.5 million, a drop of 36 per cent (see chart 4). A fall in the supply of labour on this scale should have seen the labour market position of young people improve significantly. Indeed, in the late 1980s there were serious worries that the so-called 'demographic timebomb' would result in widespread labour shortages in industries traditionally reliant on recruiting large numbers of young people. But as can be seen above, the reverse has happened: the unemployment position of young people compared with adults has worsened.

Chart 4: Fewer young people in 1990s

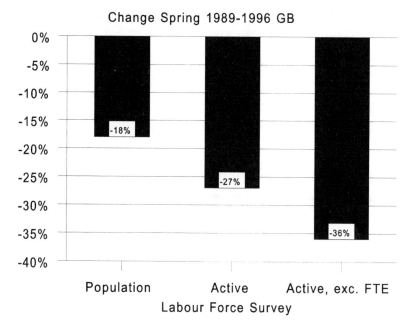

Change Spring 1989-1996 GB

If the free market economic orthodoxy was right, then a fall in the hourly earnings of young people would make young people cheaper relative to other workers, firms would demand more of them, and their unemployment rate would fall relative to the national average. Conversely, if young people became relatively more expensive than older workers, then firms would hire fewer of them and their unemployment would rise compared to the national average.

Earnings data from the New Earnings Survey shows that the opposite has happened. The earnings measure is full-time gross average hourly earnings including overtime for those on adult rates in Great Britain, for April of each year. Between April 1984 and April 1995 hourly earnings for young men fell from 82.8 per cent of the average to 73.9 per cent, while for young women hourly earnings fell from 70.5 per cent of the average to 66.3 per cent. This is shown in chart 5. Yet despite these falls the unemployment position of young people worsened when compared to the national average.

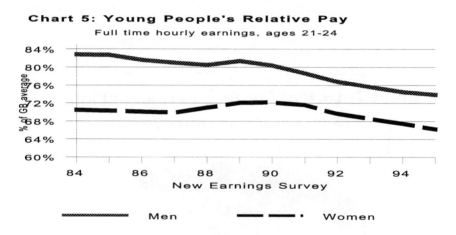

Chart 5: Young People's Relative Pay
Full time hourly earnings, ages 21-24

The same pattern emerges if hourly earnings of young men are compared with the average for all men and if the hourly earnings of young women are compared with the average for all women. This is shown in chart 6. Yet in the 1990s, young men fared worse than all men and young women fared worse than all women in terms of unemployment.

Chart 8: Male & female youth pay compared

males/females ages 21-24 as % of male/female average

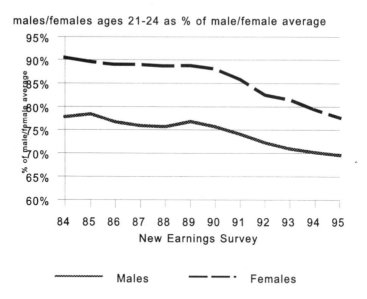

New Earnings Survey

———— Males   — — · Females

Chart 7: Lack of full-time permanent jobs in net increase in employment

Employees GB Spring 1993-96

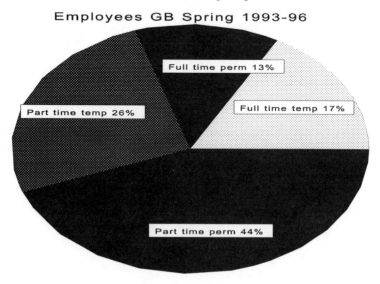

Young people and the recovery

One reason for the fall in relative earnings being combined with a worsening of the relative unemployment position of young people is the quality of job creation in this recovery, and the sort of jobs young people are often forced to take. The household Labour Force Survey shows that, comparing 1990 and 1996, the economy still had 930,000 fewer full-time employee jobs but had 540,000 more part-time employee jobs.

Moreover, there has been a remarkable increase in temporary work over the recession and into the first years of the recovery. As a result, only 13 per cent of the net increase in employment between spring 1993 and spring 1996 has been in permanent, full-time work (see chart 7).

The lack of full-time permanent jobs has meant that the 1990s have seen a rapid increase in the numbers of people in part-time or temporary work who say they want a full-time job. As figure 8 shows, between spring 1990 and spring 1996 the numbers working part-time in a main job (including the self-employed) but who wanted full-time work increased by over 120 per cent, from 350,000 or 6.3 per cent of all part-time workers to 780,000 or 12.6 per cent of all part-time workers.

FIGURE 8 : INVOLUNTARY PART-TIME AND TEMPORARY WORKING INCREASES

spring GB unadjusted 000s	spring 1990	spring 1992	spring 1996
Part-time, want full-time work	350	670	780
Temporary, want permanent work	330*	430	650

* may not be directly comparable with later estimates. Part-time is employees & self-employed.

Source: Labour Force Survey

The numbers in temporary work who want a permanent job has risen by 97 per cent, increasing from 330,000 in spring 1990 to 650,000 in spring 1996 or 42 per cent of all those in temporary employment.

Many of these new jobs are very low paid. Nearly 50 per cent of 'entry jobs' which are filled by the unemployed and new entrants to the labour force paid less than £4 an hour, and 25 per cent paid less than £3 an hour. So many of the jobs which young people take are likely to be very low paid indeed.

The latest New Earnings Survey provides information on the pay of full-time men and women and part-time women workers by age group for April 1995. The

NES shows that in April 1995 hourly median earnings (the median is the level at which exactly half earn more and half earn less) for full-time male employees aged 21-24 was £5.52 an hour.

By contrast, males between 18 and 20 had median earnings of £4.00 an hour. The corresponding figures for female full-time workers were £5.15 an hour and £3.88 an hour respectively. Female part-time employees aged 21-24 had median earnings of £3.83 an hour, female part-timers ages 18-20 had median earnings of £3.61 an hour. Earnings were much lower down the scale. The hourly earnings for those in the bottom 10 per cent and bottom 25 per cent are set out below in figure 9.

Temporary and part-time work may offer opportunities for students and young people who do not want a permanent job just yet, but most of those under 25 are likely to be looking for full-time jobs. Indeed, the Labour Force Survey shows that in spring 1996 only 13 per cent of those aged 20-24 who were ILO unemployed were looking exclusively for part-time work, compared with 16 per cent of all ILO unemployed. However, there was a significant difference between men and women - while only 7 per cent of unemployed young men ages 20-24 were exclusively looking for part-time work, 28 per cent of unemployed young women said they were looking exclusively for part-time work.

The mismatch between the sort of jobs the economy is generating and the sort of jobs people are seeking is helping keep unemployment high, and ensuring that many of those who do get a foothold in the labour market are in jobs they do not

FIGURE 9 HOURLY EARNINGS OF UNDER 25s in 1995

Ages 21-24	Lowest 10 %	Lowest 25%
Males Full-time	£3.57 or less	£4.35 or less
Females Full-time	£3.40 or less	£4.11 or less
Women Part-time	£2.77 or less	£3.21 or less
Ages 18-20		
Males Full-time	£2.60 or less	£3.28 or less
Females Full-time	£2.64 or less	£3.19 or less
Women Part-time	£2.85 or less	£3.19 or less

Note: all figures gross hourly earnings including overtime, GB, April 1995. NES estimates of hourly earnings for part-time males by age not available.
Source: New Earnings Survey

Chart 10: The sort of jobs the unemployed want

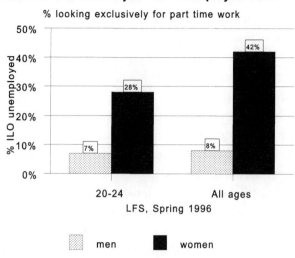

% looking exclusively for part time work

LFS, Spring 1996

□ men ■ women

really want to be in. Chart 10 shows that less than 10 per cent of young men and less than 30 per cent of young women were looking exclusively for part-time work in spring 1996.

Solutions and options

The worsening position of young people in the labour market is not confined to the UK. The Organisation for Economic Co-operation and Development (OECD) has looked at the issue of youth unemployment across a wide range of industrialised economies in the most recent *Employment Outlook*, published in June 1996. This confirmed that many of the changes identified in the above analysis in the UK - a deteriorating employment position despite falls in relative wages and a decline in supply - are taking place in other economies too.

The OECD suggests two reasons. One is that youth unemployment is very sensitive to overall economic conditions:

> As long as total unemployment remains high, it is unrealistic to expect a significant improvement in youth job prospects: both the employment and unemployment rates of young people are highly responsive to the overall state of the labour market (OECD Employment Outlook, 1996).

Youth unemployment must be tackled as part of a wider commitment to full employment, and investment in people. A sustained recovery in the labour market will see more full-time permanent jobs created. A recovery accompanied by investment in the social infrastructure - in social housing and urban regeneration - and by large-scale work and training programmes targeted on the long term unemployed would both accelerate the return of the sort of jobs the unemployed need and help ensure the sustainability of the recovery.[1]

The second reason for the poor prospects for the young unemployed suggested by the OECD is that as demand in the industrialised economies shifts towards more skilled and experienced workers, the young - and especially those without qualifications - are being left behind. Firms are preferring somewhat older and more experienced workers, even though younger workers are much cheaper. There is certainly evidence that in the UK unemployment is exceptionally low among well educated workers in the 25-34 age group (and much higher among those with less educational qualifications in the same age group).

This suggests that improvements in both vocational training and education are badly needed alongside general expansionary measures in the economy. There is now a clear danger that under present trends the national training targets set for young people and supported by government, employers and trade unions will no be met.[2]

The UK experience certainly contradicts the view that deregulation works, and the OECD study confirms that there is no evidence that the existence of minimum wages or employment protection legislation adversely affects the labour market position of those most at risk, such as the unskilled and young

---

1. The 1996 TUC Budget Submission, *A Budget for Skills and Security*, sets out some proposals in this area.
2. The Foundation Learning Targets for 2000 require:
   (a) by age 19 some 85 per cent of young people to achieve 5 GCSEs at Grade C or above, an intermediate GNVQ or an NVQ level 2;
   (b) by age 19 some 75 per cent of young people to achieve level 2 competence in communications, numeracy and IT skills; and by age 21 some 35 per cent to achieve level 3 competence;
   (c) by age 21 some 60 per cent of young people to achieve 2 GCE A levels, an advanced GNVQ or an NVQ level 3.
   The first target is likely to be achieved, progress towards the second has not been quantified, and the third is unlikely to be achieved at current rates of progress.

people. According to the OECD,

> Although economic theory indicates that wage floors can price low skill
> workers out of jobs, employment and unemployment rates for youth, women
> and unskilled workers do not appear to be significantly correlated with the
> incidence of low paid employment.

The introduction of a minimum wage would clearly benefit a disproportionately large number of young people in low paid work today, without adversely affecting their employment prospects.[3] So too would a strengthening and extension of collective bargaining in those sectors and occupations young people are concentrated in - the huge rises in inequality in the UK labour market since 1980 are partly due to the weakening of trade unions and trade union organisation.

What is very clear is that the labour market 'reforms' since 1980 have produced an almost unique increase in wage inequality in the UK economy compared with the rest of Europe, leaving the UK the low pay capital of Europe in terms of the number of low paid jobs. The loss of minimum wage protection, job security, the weakening of trade unions and the loss and reduction of welfare benefits have all contributed to this unfortunate distinction. For young people, especially those without qualifications, the social costs of these measures have been severe.

The article draws on the Labour Force Survey, an official household survey which uses definitions set down by the International Labour Organisation. Unemployment is defined as looking for work in the four weeks before the survey and being able to start a job in two weeks time. Employment is at least one hour's work a week, and includes those in full-time education. In this report, young people usually refers to the under 25s. Unless otherwise stated, all figures are for Great Britain.

---

3. *Arguments for a Minimum Wage*, TUC 1995.

New unionism in the 1990s

John Healey and Frances O'Grady

US unions are being boosted by an injection of new young energy. Could it happen here? The TUC wants to shed the image of unions as exclusive institutions for the middle-aged male.

One evening last October, 2000 young Americans crowded into the library of Columbia University, New York, to hear union leader John Sweeney appeal for their help in revitalising the US labour movement.

It was standing room only for what was billed as 'A Teach-In with the labour movement'. As the first of ten workshop-based events held around the US organised by students, academics and unions turnout far exceeded expectations. Media commentators described the atmosphere as 'electric'. And Sweeney, who became leader of the AFL-CIO - the US TUC - a couple of years ago, was joined on the platform by veteran feminist writer Betty Friedan and Harvard professor of African-American studies Cornel West. He was treated to a standing ovation.

As one student, Michelle Sieff, explained to the *New York Times*: 'Students are reaching for something right now. There's a lot of apathy, as we all know, but there's a desire to find an alternative to the MBA-law school track of life.' For the new generation of American students, organised labour is fast becoming as potent a cause as Vietnam was for their parents in the 1960s. Union Summer, the AFL-CIO's campaign to 'blitz' the low-wage Sun Belt last summer, enlisted over a thousand college student volunteers to help organise new members. And the AFL-CIO's Organising Institute which was set up in 1989 has now trained over six hundred young people to create a formidable 'cadre' of dedicated union organisers.

Anti-union bosses in the US may make their British counterparts look like amateurs, but the problems bedevilling the US labour movement sound all too familiar to British ears. Union membership has been in steady decline for a number of years. Unemployment, hostile laws and casualisation conspire to make the job of even the best union organiser a tough one. And this side of the Atlantic, trade unionists are waking up to the idea that while new rights to representation and recognition would make a difference, getting Tony Blair into Number 10 is no more a guarantee of membership growth than having Bill Clinton in the White House has proved to be in the States.

The American labour movement is at a turning point. Sweeney's presidency marks a rejection of business unionism in favour of social activism. The AFL-CIO's robust campaigning on issues such as the minimum wage would have been unimaginable in the days of cold war conservatism. The organising fervour of the new leadership has succeeded in capturing the imagination and commitment of a whole new generation of young people. The million dollar question for British unions is, could it happen here?

At first sight the prospects look bleak. British union membership records reveal few signs of organised resistance to the rough treatment meted out to young workers. Although the problem of low union density among young workers is not new. But the scale of the problem is growing, and it is no exaggeration to suggest that the union movement is in danger of losing a generation. Just one in five of the under-25s at work hold a union card, a figure which falls to six per cent of those under 20.

Yet young people in Britain are at the sharp end of today's labour market. The jobless rate is double that of older workers, pay rates barely top two-thirds and young workers are three times more likely to be on temporary contracts (see Ian Brinkley's contribution in this issue). Surely they should be ripe for unionisation?

Testament of youth

If unions are going to solve this puzzle, then we have to see the problem more clearly. The TUC report, *Testament of Youth*, based on a survey of over 1000 18-24 year-olds carried out by MORI, aimed to find out from young people themselves how they felt about work, unions and life.

Contrary to common 'couldn't-care-less' stereotypes, our research shows that young people care passionately about doing interesting and worthwhile work. They want the chance to learn new skills, and they want to be respected for what they do. The harsh reality, however, is that one in three earn less than £100 a week, more than half complain of unfair treatment at work, and nearly three-quarters don't qualify for protection against unfair dismissal.

They are individually optimistic about their own future but deeply pessimistic for their generation. Just eleven per cent think the quality of life for young people in Britain will improve in the next year, while 15 per cent believe job prospects will get better. With the recent dips in official statistics, unemployment may be fast disappearing from public view. But for young people it is far from being a problem of the past. Over half of young people (53 per cent) - including over half of Conservative supporters - see unemployment as the most important issue facing Britain today.

With only two in five saying they are very likely to vote in the next general election, there's widespread apathy about politics and disregard for politicians. More than two-thirds don't believe politicians know what working life today is really like. But if young people are sceptical of politicians, they're sympathetic to unions. More than half believe trade union leaders do know what working life is like, sixty per cent agree unions are essential to protect people's interests at work and one third say they would join a union if they were asked.

The heart of the problem, of course, is that we're not asking them. We're not even getting basic information to them. Eighty-six per cent of young people say they know nothing or not very much about trade unions, and even amongst current union members more than half feel ill-informed. So, overcoming ignorance, rather than hostility, is the challenge unions face.

We can be confident that young people share many of our basic values and support the things unions stand for. There is strong backing for new rights at work among 18-24 year-olds: 78 per cent want a minimum wage, 80 per cent say employers who don't train their staff should be made to do so, 86 per cent agree part-timers should have the same rights in law as full-timers and 90 per cent believe all employees should have the legal right to be represented if they've got problems with their employer.

Traditionally, discontent is seen as the recruiting agent for unions. But, when it comes to young people, are unions making the right pitch? The TUC carried out a separate survey of unions to find out whether the bargaining issues they identified as priorities for young people matched the concerns young people themselves expressed.

Unions came up with the right answers - but in the wrong order. According to the survey, unions see the most important concern for young people as being training/education (58 per cent), followed by job security and pay (both at 53 per cent). But when young people are asked to name ways in which their jobs could be improved, 'a pay increase' outstrips any other concern by more than two to one. Improved pay (53 per cent), better hours (18 per cent) and increased training (10 per cent) are the top three priorities mentioned by young people themselves.

This is not to suggest that union priorities should slavishly follow the latest opinion poll findings. At the bargaining table, unions have to represent the interests of the whole membership and not just any one section. And there may be good strategic reasons for protecting, for example, the ideal of the steady job, even if many young people - especially those without caring responsibilities at the teenage end of the spectrum - see it as an overrated virtue. But the patent mismatch between what young people say they want and what unions think they ought to want should at least provoke serious debate.

Again, when young people are asked what is important to them in a job, 'decent pay' tops the league at 56 per cent, followed by having 'an interesting an enjoyable job' (51 per cent) and 'the chance to learn new skills' (41 per cent). Feeling valued and respected at work is key to many young people - especially school leavers and young women. One third (33 per cent) of all young people mention a 'boss who respects you' as an important factor they look for in a job. One young respondent explained what respect at work means to her: 'They treat you as a person, they ask you to do things, they don't tell you to do them'.

If pay is a crude but critical measure of the value British society places on its citizens, then young people's respect rating has slumped. Since their exemption from the wages council system, and its subsequent abolition, young people employed in those industries which were protected have seen their earning power fall relative to the national average.

Bargaining campaigns run by some unions to win a basic payrate of £4/hour and the TUC-wide demand for a national minimum wage have the potential to win active popular support - especially from the one in three of young people stuck in dead end jobs paying under £5000 a year. Raising the profile of these campaigns and sharpening their appeal to young people could act as a powerful recruitment tool.

The New Unionism programme

Reaching young workers is a key theme of the TUC's New Unionism project launched last November. New Unionism aims to put the drive for membership growth at the top of unions' agenda and create a new organising culture. The project is marked by a determination to face up to the membership slide which has seen union density fall from around half of the workforce when the Tories took power in 1979 to just under a third today. Its message is that the rise of the non-unionised sector poses a much greater threat than any inter-union rivalry. Unions can no longer afford - if indeed they ever could - to fight each other chasing the same few members in an ever shrinking pool of traditional strongholds.

The New Unionism strategy is underpinned by a number of key principles:

- *Put organising first* Recruitment and organisation must become the top priority for the whole union movement.
- *Invest real resources* Organising doesn't come cheap - only a significant commitment of resources - money *and* people - to recruitment and organisation can reverse membership decline.
- *Develop a strategic approach* Properly thought out and resourced organising campaigns which set realistic targets are more likely to deliver results - and boost morale.
- *Cut out wasteful rivalries* Unions must be encouraged to focus on the rise of a non-unionised sector and the threat this poses to the whole union movement.
- *Like recruits like* Organisers must reflect the diversity of the workforce we aim to unionise, and those groups traditionally under-represented in unions.
- *Increase the use of dedicated organisers - and boost their training and status.* The AFL-CIO Organising Institute and Australian ACTU Organising Works programmes have brought new blood into the movement, upskilled the job of organising - and paid for themselves through recruitment success.
- *Build lay representatives' confidence and skills* Investing in building lay representatives' organisation helps strengthen existing bases and free up full-time officers to organise in new areas.

- *Communications are key* Imaginative campaigning and use of the mass media are key to getting the union message across to working people.
- *Government sympathy does not guarantee growth* Union membership can continue to slide even where the government in power is sympathetic to union values and, as in Australia, a social partnership Accord is in place.

The TUC task group steering the New Unionism project has agreed a work programme, including the development of special organising projects, and piloting an AFL-CIO-style 'academy' to train up - mainly young - dedicated organisers sponsored by unions. The challenge for trade unions aiming to organise young workers is two-fold. First, to provide the vision that things can be changed and that exploitation at work is not inevitable. And second, to prove that unions can protect the 'new workers' effectively - and that there aren't no-go areas for union organisation.

It will not be enough to introduce a student subs rate or set up a youth committee. As a recent TUC women's conference discussion document noted: 'For those outside our movement, unions seem bureaucratic, cumbersome, male and boring.' Add to that list 'middle-aged' and we have a succinct description of how potential - and many existing - young members may see unions. We have to put unions in front of young people through schools, sports, music festivals, campaign events, careers fairs, job search initiatives, advice lines and the Internet. And it can be done - the TUC's *Respect* festival run in 1996 drew 80,000 young people to London's Finsbury Park.

Profile and recruitment are only part of the answer. If we are to avoid creating a revolving-door membership we need to tackle the problem of involvement too. A number of unions are now creating alternative paths to participation, alongside the traditional youth committee approach, from music festivals to the launch of youth activist networks. Unions could also learn from other social movements, including the direct action techniques deployed by the lesbian and gay group Outrage and by environmental campaigns, and the community-based approach of some anti-racist organisations.

Nor will it be enough to confine our efforts to areas with established union recognition, as most young people now work in sectors with low levels of unionisation. TUC labour market analysis suggests that the critical issue affecting unionisation is not so much how old you are, but where you work. Over one third of young workers are in the distribution, hotels and catering sector, and a further third are employed in sales and personal service jobs.

In the short term some unions are likely to concentrate their energies on building existing bases. With around half of the workforce covered by union recognition agreements, but less than a third in a union, there is plenty of scope to 'mop up' softer targets - and build morale as well as membership. But if we are to organise 'new' workers and help tackle growing inequality, unions can not neglect the tougher targets where young people are more likely to be found.

Breaking new ground is an uphill struggle. Often, union organising initiatives are caught in the crossfire between casualisation and bully boy management tactics. While union membership enhances job security at a national level, in hard to organise areas union representatives are sometimes sitting targets for the sack. Yet the chances against proving victimisation in an industrial tribunal are around two to one.

High turnover, fuelled by an increase in temporary contracts and low pay, also serve to make union organisation fragile. The annual staff turnover of so-called 'crews' in some fast food chains is approaching 400 per cent. Even if winning recognition was not a problem, unions would need to sustain a permanent recruitment campaign to maintain membership.

Tackling 'greenfield' sites or industries is a daunting exercise but those unions developing a longer term strategic approach are finding that there are paler shades of green. Tracking company ownership and suppliers, contracted out and out-sourced employees can create pathways into non-organised workplaces. Developing closer links with students and the NUS - whose members increasingly have to earn while they learn - could also be productive. A shift in the power imbalance between employers and workers through the creation of new rights will help too. But ultimately there will need to be a significant and sustained investment of resources - finance and people - if unions are to make a lasting impression.

The first wave New Unionism pioneers succeeded in organising casual, women and young workers on an unprecedented scale at the end of the last century. We've done it for previous generations. We have to do it again for the next.

The first of a series of UK union teach-ins takes place at the University of North London on 24 October. It is organised jointly with the university by the TUC and NUS.

Lawrence & Wishart invite you to join **The LW Club**. Launched to mark our 60th anniversary, the LW Club offers more than a conventional book club. As well as all new L&W paperback titles, **LW Club** members receive special discounts to a wide range of conferences and events, and discounts on all L&W backlist titles.

You can become a member of the LW Club for **just £15.00 quarterly**. As an **LW Club** member you will receive **absolutely free all new paperback books** on publication* (approximately 10 - 15 pa. - *at cover price this would average £160.00pa*). Upon joining you will receive a free book chosen by you (see below) **.

LW CLUB MEMBERSHIP INCLUDES

All New Lawrence & Wishart Paperbacks FREE*

as they are published, a constant source of rewarding and intellectually stimulating reading.

Free tickets for conferences/ events

sponsored by **Lawrence & Wishart**, including the popular Signs of the Times annual conference, various book launches, and all New Times events.

Discounts on conferences

including the annual Unions conference organised by Democratic Left, and the Signs of the Times seminar series.

Exclusive discounts on all L&W titles

the chance to purchase any L&W paperback or hardback title published prior to your membership at a 35% discount.

Free catalogue and bookmarks

plus a quarterly newsletter with details of forthcoming publications; details of journals, New Times books, website offers; letters and a special feature.

And we hope you will join us at our **Christmas events**.

Early applications for membership will receive a **free t-shirt** featuring the popular route map from *The Green London Way* (While stocks last).

For further details, membership application form & **FREE** catalogue write to:
L&W, 99a Wallis Road, London E9 5LN.
Tel: 0181-533 2506 Fax: 0181-533 7369 E-mail: l-w-bks.demon.co.uk

*This excludes journals

** Free book list includes: *You Tarzan: Masculinity Movies and Men*, Janet Thumim & Pat Kirkham (eds); *Activating Theory: Lesbian, Gay, Bisexual Politics*, Joseph Bristow & Angelia Wilson (eds); *Black Tribunes: Black Political Participation in Britain*, Terri Sewell.

Paradigm lost?
Youth and pop in the 90s
Rupa Huq

*Youth culture in the 1990s has been redefining itself
around two vibrant musical forms - dance and
Britpop.*

> Rock, initially at any rate, was a contemporary incitement to mindless fucking
> and arbitrary vandalism: screw and smash music.
>
> George Melly, *Revolt into Style*

Throughout its existence pop has been an essential part of British post-war youth
culture: a cathartic outlet for youthful self-expression, empowerment and liberation
from adult culture. Encapsulated in the Who lyric 'hope I die before I get old', pop
mythology has dictated the value of dying young and beautiful. (Although the
Who never lived up to their stated aim.) When slacker king Kurt Cobain did die
young he was elevated to youth icon status, helped by his suicide declaration - 'it's
better to burn than fade away'. Pop has always been young because sound and fury
equate with youth; quiet signifies maturity; and ultimately silence denotes death.
But today pop's assured place at the core of youth culture seems precarious. Youth
culture is undergoing profound changes. In an ironic reversal, four decades of pop
history means that it is steeped in the past: the subject of numerous books,
publications and even university degrees. The pop-youth cohort is increasingly
difficult to sustain; pop's audience has become more than teenage malcontents. In
1995 Simon Frith, founder of the 'sociology of rock' commented: 'age is a funny
thing in music. For young people now, rock and roll is old people's music.'[1] Indeed,

---

1. 'Rock of Ages', interview with Simon Frith by David Walker, *Times Higher Education
   Supplement*, 1.12.95.

so much so that 'pop is dead' has now become a fashionable line to take.

The case for pop's demise was advanced in the early 1990s in both popular culture and academic discourse. For example, former punk journalist turned television cultural commentator Tony Parsons announced the 'death of pop' in *The Times* (21.11.92). In evidence Parsons cited radio stations based on the contradiction of 'nostalgia pop', tribute bands, computer games, music sales through jeans commercials, the ascendance of Australian soaps and the creative bankruptcy of current music in its revivalism and dehumanising technologies. Critics in the 1990s argue that rock/pop no longer offers escapism or reacts against the system, because it's been subsumed by the dominant culture. US academic Camille Paglia invoked the generation X stereotype when she claimed in 1992: 'rock is a victim of its own success ... White suburban youth, rock's main audience, is trapped in creature comforts. They no longer have direct contact with folk music, blues, the oral repositories of love, hate, suffering and redemption.'

Examples of pop's new found respectability were rife. The annual Mercury Music Prize and the Brit Awards illustrate the passage from anti-establishment to arch-establishment. Big prize money and commercial sponsors have reduced pop to a competitive sport. Pop magazines aimed at the older post-music-press pop fan seemed also to deepen an erosion of pop's natural correspondence with youth. In 1993, following the success of Q magazine's formula of rock retrospective and stereo equipment review for the discerning (i.e. older) reader, came *Mojo* for post Q readers. A rash of 'classic' artists was relaunched for a younger, although not an altogether unsuspecting audience. From the grave emerged Jimi Hendrix and the Doors, their respective careers transformed from discarded back-catalogue acts to chart successes. Such acts were the antithesis of the rock and roll animal: never late, never answering back and never hung over. The technology of digital remastering has accelerated the process. Pop becomes a complete body of work, sold in box sets, subject of its own encyclopaedias like opera or classical music. The Velvet Underground and the Sex Pistols punctured their one-time mystique by reforming. The fruits of the Pistols tour was released on CD to mop up the consumers unlucky(?) enough not to attend, faster than you could say the words Great Rock and Roll Swindle.

The study of pop has found its disciplinal home under the rubric of cultural studies. However pop's defining characteristics of spontaneity and youthful allure are to an extent undermined when it becomes the stuff of tutorials and lecture halls, promoted by the Friths and Paglias. This academicisation is a two-way process. For some years the distinction between rock journalism and academic criticism has been blurring, with the rise of anthropologically influenced 'style journalism' as exemplified by *The Face*. Jon Savage's writing has appeared in the *New Left Review*, Sunday supplements and the music magazines. Tony Parsons has spent the 1990s arguing that there were no more heroes alongside Oxbridge dons on BBC2 and Channel 4 arts programmes. A 1994 advert for his newspaper, *The Telegraph*, showed him in a megastore being mobbed by a crowd of adoring girls.

Pop culture's demise can also be observed when its products rise to political prominence. Tony Blair, having once played in a student band, attached himself to rock symbolism by appearing with U2 at the *Q* music awards in 1995. The arguments of such nostradamuses of pop are in a large degree imprisoned in their authors' own age-centred prejudices, which create a 'things ain't what they used to be' generation gap. Media clichés about 1990s youth - the slackers and generation X - provide a negative to the nostalgic coverage of the anniversaries of Woodstock and the Isle of Wight festival. Yet the notion of pop music's centrality to previous generations is itself a falsity. The Summer of Love did not impact on everyone equally. Many young people were completely untouched by it. And even accepting the 1960s orthodoxy of the pop-youth paradigm, there is no reason to assume that new generations will follow suit. Young people in the 1990s have increasing means at their disposal to attain youth culture's eternal goals. There is not one unitary youth culture but many: ravers, techno, cyberpunk, indie kids, goth, junglaists, grunge, bhangra, ragga, internet junkies and even ... squares. If we take rock to be music which is guitar based, with melodies of regular pace, perhaps it *is* dead - or perhaps is being replaced by other entities: variations on a theme. After all transience and ephemerality are an important feature of contemporary musical forms and youth culture.

Rave on: 90s dance

Rave has been ominously labelled the last subculture. In media circles much of the early 1990s was spent scrabbling around in a quest for the 'new rock and roll' (alternative cabaret, cyberspace, etc). The candidate that seemed most likely was 90s dance music, even though it was regarded as a sign of the end of pop itself. Other 'death of pop' allegations have been aimed at cultural forms which have displaced pop's force, but dance music is different, because all of its offspring -

techno, hard house, handbag house, ambient, hardcore, jungle, drum and bass, intelligent house, Goa trance and what London's *Time Out* calls 'other moves and grooves' - are original musical forms.

Rave is the event to which the techno-based soundtrack is added. Yet the received wisdom of 'music' and 'the song' has led to claims that techno isn't music at all. This is rooted in the received wisdom of 'music' and 'the song'. Indeed techno does break all the conventions. The beats per minute rating of a track is crucial. The composer passes other people's music through a sampler to be reconstituted anew. Techno does not even rely on regular musical notation, it is recorded straight onto tape, bypassing the need for additional musicians to play other parts. Punk DIY is updated for the 1990s, substituting the guitar and three chords for a pile of records and a mixing desk. Techno is the ultimate 'be-there' joke: mood music which is meaningless when divorced from its context. Few would listen to nine hours of uninterrupted techno at home, yet it makes perfect sense at a rave. Techno is anonymous, contrasting sharply with the usually accepted 'social' function of music making and performance from its folk roots. Rave contradicts the spectacle of the pop concert. DJs are known by reputation alone: the name Carl Fox or Fabio on a flyer will attract audiences who wouldn't recognise their hero even if they fell over him in the bottled water queue.

Britpop (vs dance): problematics/politics

If dance is devoid of personalities, Britpop has thrived on them. Oasis and Blur's 'Who's the greatest?' phoney war made *Newsnight* in the Summer of 1995. In April 1996 Jarvis Cocker of Pulp raised eyebrows with his stage invasion of Michael Jackson's performance at the Brit Awards. The same summer Oasis's laddish antics nudged aside world affairs in UK news coverage. In Britpop 'working-class and hard' has been a desirable attribute. Middle class bands such as Suede (Haywards Heath, Sussex) and Blur (Colchester, Essex) have thus seen fit to appropriate cockney accents (mockney) and intonation in their singing voices. The lineage of ostentatious laddishness with the eye on 'looking good' can be traced back to the 1980s 'casual'. But despite the macho image Britpop has also encouragingly produced a number of strong female role models: Elastica's Justine Frischman, Sleeper's Louise Weiner and Echobelly's Sonia Madan, who is also Asian. These performers are outspoken in interview. Their assertive, upfront posturing is reflected in the slogan 'girl power' which symbolises sexual confidence. This attitude has also informed the hugely successful Spice Girls. Girl power is unlike the old style feminism - or at least the negative features associated with it - because it substitutes hedonism for austerity. Nevertheless it is a liberated hedonism which wouldn't have been possible without *The Female Eunuch*.

The issue of lads and gender has not been Britpop's only problematic. From the point of view of ethnicity, Britpop is resolutely white. Mark Fisher argued in the *New Statesman* that Britpop was the musical equivalent of John Major's back to basics vision of an England of the village green, warm beer and spinsters cycling to communion.[2] Indeed, in some respects Britpop exhibits a 'little Englander' cultural introversion and regression back to a mythologised past. It minimises black influences in its music, in tune with the contemporary discrediting of the principle of multiculturalism. Elsewhere it has been claimed that Britpop is close in philosophy to New Labour: selective amnesia, reinvention and a denial of past roots. Politicians themselves have not been slow to exploit the element of nationalism in Britpop. Tony Blair adopted an Ian Broudie lyric for his leader's speech at the Labour Party Conference in 1996 ('Football's coming home' deftly converted to a jubilant 'Labour's coming home'). And John Redwood, writing in *The Guardian*, claimed that Britpop was a healthy sign of Conservative Britain, again seizing on an Ian Broudie and Lightening Seeds couplet - 'The future's blue/ lucky you'.

However, leaving aside the fact that Oasis themselves are the sons of Irish immigrants, there is more to Britpop than straight, white boys blindly committed to the glorification of guitars and Englishness. Irony and playfulness are also present. The celebration of Britain in Blur's work is more of a love / hate relationship with Blighty, as suggested in their album title *Modern Life is rubbish* . Pulp's witty and perceptive 1996 Mercury Music prize-winning *Different Class* owed as much to British kitchen sink cinema and realist fiction as it did to pop's past.

Unlike Britpop, dance music and jungle in particular do represent a more internationalist outlook. Rave in practice is intrinsically European. Its music includes Belgian new beat, Frankfurt techno and has drawn on gay disco. The Love parade in Berlin is established as the leading world rave event. But its theory is wider: drawing on source material that embraces world music, bhangra

2. Mark Fisher 'Indie Reactionaries *New Statesman and Society*, 7.7.95.

(the product of second generation Asian youth), and the utopian dream of the drug paradise Goa. Other roots have been traced back to Stonehenge and the Druids. These multiple sources of inspiration have encouraged the idea of rave culture as the 'coming together of tribes'. The paganism-meets-technology of the 'free party' ravers prides itself on an ill-defined loosely anti-capitalist manifesto, as evidenced in the anti-Criminal Justice Bill movement. However tribalism is not without its problems. Many white crusty ravers and road protesters, with dreadlocks and living in trees, identify with the 'primitive way of life', acting out the fantasy of Goa tourism that would be unrecognisable to most people of tribal societies. Their attitude recalls the Sex Pistols barb 'a cheap holiday in other people's misery'.

'Britpop and Dance are on the same side: original 90s pop music by the young, for the young'

Despite its claims to be an alternative lifestyle, dance is caught in that inescapable element of youth cultures: commercialism. Subcultures start with the genuine innovators at their 'purest' underground moment. Then the multifarious tentacles of the youth culture industries get hold of them, in the scramble to 'cash in'; the advent of techno being played in supermarkets signals the move from street culture to high street culture. A three day festival in Oxfordshire staged by the commercial outfit Universe Promotions even called itself 'Tribal Gathering' - which sat incongruously with the £25 a head ticket charge. Britpop is, arguably more deeply immersed than dance in international capital. For the British music industry it provided a badly needed revival of its fortunes after the demise of grunge. Of the $32 billion global music market in 1996, 16 per cent of ownership rested with Sony whose umbrella sheltered Oasis (Sony owns 59 per cent of Oasis' supposedly 'independent' base Creation Records), a 14 per cent share was held by Polygram whose subsidiary Island is home to Pulp, and a further 13 per cent was owned by EMI who include Blur (on subdivision Food records).[3] Noel Gallagher's (Oasis) tirade against the 'corporate pigs' of the music industry at the 1996 Brit Awards seemed to express a recognition of the inbuilt tension between pop's market-economic dimension and the receivers of its texts, the consumer; and to raise the question of who is leading who.

---

3. Figures from 'Who Calls the Tune' *Observer* 25.2.96.

Some concluding thoughts

Whether dance or Britpop is more popular is irrelevant. For Britpop, attitude is crucial. It has few original features of musical merit; guitar power-chords and string sections in pop are hardly novel. Dance music, on the other hand has demonstrated a lasting influence amongst Britain's young since at least the appearance of Acid House in 1987. However Britpop has the edge in terms of personalities and sales. Indeed in recent years the British music industry has struck a high note in the UK's balance of payments deficit. The two musical forms have much in common. Both can be seen as intrinsically postmodern. Dance's use of technology via the process of sampling is a cause and effect of pop's modern tendency to use fragments of its own past imagination in new ways. Brit pop's creation of perfect pop, reworking punk and the 1960s into its tapestry, is another consequence of the rich reference points now available to the pop retrospectivist. Britpop *v* Dance is of little importance because both are on the same side: original 90s pop music by the young, for the young, against the aged voices of reaction who attack youth.

But classifying pop's audience as exclusively 'youth', once historically valid, is now inaccurate. However this is not an automatic cause for pop's obituary. Pop is now only one component of a complex equation of youth culture (di)versions competing for the leisure time of young people. Despite fears of pop being supplanted by cyberspace it is important to remember that new technologies are cumulative, existing alongside rather than superseding one another. This was the case with video music, which in MTV can even be seen to have enriched pop; as CD Rom and the Internet have the potential to do. Britpop, for all its problematic ethnicity and musical unoriginality, has proved to be an interesting spectator sport. And although much dance music is indeed genre defying if one takes traditional categories as a basis for description, our thinking should be wider than this. New musical forms require new categorisations. To pitch Britpop against dance in a dichotomous 'village green *v* urban jungle' battle, as the press have done, fails to realise that there is room for both in pop's broad church, and indeed for other facets to exist.

90s music has been criticised for its apoliticalness: the hippie mantra 'all you need is love' and the punk war cry 'anarchy in the UK' is replaced by 'rave on'. Pop reflects its time and this can be seen as a rejection of naivety for realism. The musical resistance to the Criminal Justice Bill arguably mobilised with more youthful vigour than the corporate Band Aid. Today, any new street originating style (for want of a better term) will be characterised by the extent to which it exists within the shadow of its own past, precisely because it now has a past - five decades worth. In the 1990s pop music has reached an unparalleled visibility in the UK. The position of youth and pop can be summarised best (with apologies to Stevie Smith) as 'raving not drowning'.

'That's entertainment'
Generation X in the time of New Labour

Michael Kenny

Mike Kenny argues that youth disaffection is part of a wider picture of social fragmentation.

One of the most salient features of Tony Blair's political style since he assumed the leadership of the Labour Party has been his repeated deployment of a distinctively generational symbolism. The imagery of a 'young Britain' about to be born once the yoke of Conservative rule is thrown off recurs throughout Labour's public rhetoric. Indeed Blair's own political image is frequently cast in the mould of the fresh-faced newcomer, not worn down by the cynicism of his elders or grooved in the routines of political life. This stance allows him to present himself as up-to-date in his thinking, and in tune with the political Zeitgeist. It was no accident, then, that he accepted the invitation to appear at the 'Brit' awards in 1995 and has happily revealed his, fairly eclectic, contemporary musical tastes.

In fact, Blair's generational identity is more complicated than his self-image suggests. After he gained the leadership his biography was the subject of intense media speculation, which focused especially on his (lack of) misdemeanors as a student in the 'swinging' sixties. Not only has he withstood this scrutiny in personal terms, but he has played a clever game concerning this most troublesome and symbolic of decades. With an authenticity that only a 1960s survivor could muster, he has solemnly refuted the excessive libertarianism of the political culture spawned in these years whilst simultaneously gesturing towards more 'liberal' views on questions such as gay rights and racial prejudice. Blair's relationship to the 1960s, and to different aspects of modern political and social culture, is deeply ambiguous and politically 'managed'. In this, as in other respects, he clearly echoes that other political baby-boomer - Bill Clinton - whose identity has also been carved out against this most troubling and difficult of decades.

The politics of generational symbolism is integral to Blair's appeal. In general he has played a highly self-conscious game, seeking to take his appeal to groups of potential voters whom the Labour Party might otherwise have failed to capture. The party has gained a raft of new, younger members since his accession to the leadership, a development he has sought to build upon by appointing a Youth spokesperson and creating a new task force. Simultaneously he has proved sensitive to some of the most important underlying social trends of the day. As Geoff Mulgan and Helen Wilkinson have argued, there is an important connection between a fairly pervasive disillusion with politics and the disenchantment of young people in particular, which most politicians do not recognise.[1] Blair has shown signs of trying to bridge this divide, taking his message to milieux and media where the political parties have generally failed to go.

But the attempt to capture more votes from younger people will not of itself address the profound disaffection which many feel towards the political system. The problem of youthful alienation from official political processes is unlikely to be solved by showing a more open attitude to the new information technologies or appearing on the right TV programmes. This is because this particular issue is merely the tip of a large iceberg made up of interconnected and longstanding problems. These include the questions of how to integrate younger generations into the political systems of modern states; when adulthood is deemed to begin in social and political terms; how to secure the legitimacy of states in the context of continuous generational change; and, finally, how the political systems of contemporary states should aggregate the different needs and interests of an increasingly fluid and apparently unpredictable population.

Whilst the question of youth alienation from the political process has been much discussed, the interconnections between this and other contemporary concerns has

1. Geoff Mulgan and Helen Wilkinson, *Freedom's Children*, Demos Publications, London, 1995.

been missed. In particular, we need to consider the increasingly problematic nature of the 'adulthood' offered to the young. Adult men and women have in the last thirty years experienced profound dislocations in terms of the kinds of roles society delineates - for example as carers, workers and lovers; these 'social' roles were often assumed to underpin the 'political' identities expressed through party allegiance and ideological affiliation, though reality was always different from this. But as a range of changes have eroded and redefined these social roles, they have become the sites of intense argument and social conflict. These developments on the lives of adults in general cannot be separated from the discussion of 'Generation X'.

'The politics of generational symbolism is integral to Blair's appeal'

The crisis of young people's political participation and enthusiasm is not a blip on the political horizon. Rather, it should be considered as organically connected with a set of other debates and concerns - about moral authority in the home and the classroom, the politics of parenting and the propensity of some young men to anti-social behaviour in public places. Understanding these different questions as being related helps us to perceive why the world of adulthood in general appears so fraught and unappealing to those about to reach it. On the political left, the question of the 'socialisation' of children into the social world of adults has been addressed by a range of different theorists from varying traditions. But a wide gulf exists on this question. On the one hand, critics influenced by thinkers ranging from Foucault to Marcuse, have emphasised the repression and disruption to the individual's personality occasioned by learning the routines of conventional adult life. On the other, the morally conservative agenda of some in the contemporary Labour Party stigmatises young people as disorderly and threatening - in need of the 'discipline' imparted by paid labour, and a dose of moral correction. A vast space exists between these poles, in which more affirmative and sophisticated ideas about what socialisation could and should mean in the twenty-first century need to be explored.

The passage of young men and women into adulthood, in both social and political senses, has also been problematised by the development of specifically youthful sub-cultural styles and enclaves. As Bill Osgerby shows, the emergence of youth-orientated popular culture can be traced back to the pre-war period, but was most marked and controversial during the 1950s, the decade of affluence and supposed 'classlessness'. With the emergence of the teenager and other youth styles, the gap between young people and the established political system was semi-institutionalised. Commentators in the 1950s were as concerned about the apparent proliferation of new 'lifestyles' for the young - vicariously explored in Colin MacInnes' novels of segments of London life - as are many today. They also connected these developments with changes in the political realm: some 'revisionist' thinkers, for example, interpreted Labour's succession of election defeats, in 1951, 1955 and 1959 as in part the result of the loss of a hold over the younger generation.[2]

Modern states have continuously sought to establish institutional routes whereby the young can be socialised into the culture and practices of political citizenship, in ways, that complement prevailing notions of adulthood. The 'intermediate' institutions of civil society - schools, community organisations, pubs, churches and familial structures - have played important roles, channelling social aspirations and shaping identities so that the young learn and reproduce the civic values and shared meanings of the communities in which they live. But it seems that the value systems taught by these institutions no longer enjoy the consensus that they once did, leading cultural conservatives to lament the growth of relativism and pluralism, and 'radicals' to question the wisdom of 'traditional' values in contemporary circumstances. There are several different episodes in this complex story of de-legitimation, including the challenges issued by the claims of new social groups and identities from the early 1960s, and the effects of the unleashing of market forces in the 1980s.

The decline of the values disseminated by some of Britain's most longstanding institutions has contributed to the erosion of traditional models of masculinity and femininity, propelling a host of new issues on to the political agenda, from the politics of parenting to young male violence. The world of work has long been one of the most important locations where prevailing notions of social and political citizenship were learned. But the institutionalisation of long-term unemployment as well as the deskilling of many young people in the contemporary labour market mean that this arena no longer functions in this way. Those who can find jobs

2. Anthony Crosland, *The Future of Socialism*, Macmillan, New York 1957.

frequently work in low-paid and poorly unionised sectors, where traditional forms of allegiance and solidarity have more or less disappeared. (see the article by John Healey and Francis O'Grady in this issue). According to Mulgan and Wilkinson, only a third of 16-24 year olds have a union at their workplace, whilst only 42 per cent who have the option have joined one.[3]

The declining legitimacy of institutions like the church, schools and familial structures and the values associated with them is undoubtedly connected with young people's disaffection with mainstream politics. This is expressed through low voter turn-out rates and the decline in youth membership of the main parties. Recent opinion surveys reveal high levels of cynicism: only 4 per cent of 15-35 year olds, in a Mori poll, felt that politicians were doing a good job of maintaining moral standards. A social attitude survey devoted to the views of young people found that 59 per cent of those questioned professed little or no interest in politics.[4]

The political parties have tried different ways of orchestrating the allegiances of the younger sections of their populations, and have frequently found it hard to command sustained loyalty over the medium or longer term. In Britain they have relied heavily upon semi-autonomous youth organisations for these purposes. Interestingly, some common features characterise the history of these bodies in the two main parties. At different times they have become too autonomous and rebellious in relation to their parent organisations, most spectacularly in the case of the Federation of Conservative Students and the Young Socialists in the Labour Party. The constitutional and political roles allotted to these bodies were the product of an uneasy compromise between the more instrumental concerns of the party hierarchies and wider principles of party organisation which granted relative independence to separate constituencies. Student political organisations too have often become the venues for internecine power struggles rather than creative collective action. Not surprisingly these have provided an ideal training ground for hardened political operators. Frequently beset by the cultures of sectarianism, political manipulation and careerism, the youth organisations of political parties long ago ceased to be

---

3. Mulgan and Wilkinson, *op cit*, p38.
4. *Politics and Voting: a briefing paper published by the British Youth Council*, London, 1995; and D.Walker, 'Young people, politics and the media', in *Young People's Social Attitudes*, Barnados Publishing, London, p121.

meaningful spaces for political debate or sources of initiative and ideas for the parent party. In fact, as was most spectacularly evident in the case of the FCS in the Conservative Party in the 1980s, they at time became self-parodies - the sources of embarrassment rather than strength.

In terms of young voters, parties have made several attempts to adopt the emblems and styles of popular culture and fashion, and hook up with currents in youth culture, especially pop music. The Red Wedge project of the mid-1980s was one of the more interesting examples of this politics, whilst the recent Rock the Vote initiative, imported from the US, is designed to increase voting rates amongst the young. But such efforts have always proved short-lived, and seem in certain respects to run counter to the tides of contemporary social change. For instance, in a culture that increasingly prides itself upon diversity, the notion of a cultural politics which fixes the loyalty of its devotees to one party seems anachronistic. Equally, the complexity and relative autonomy of sub-cultural styles and practices means that the public sphere is not so much rejected as bypassed within the cultural structures of youthful life. Thus there are areas in which young people are relatively culturally empowered, yet the 'capital' they derive from these are as - sporting activities, surfing the net or making music - means little in the wider social world. And whilst civil society has become more dense and fissiparous, the public domain has in many ways become detached from the institutions and cultures which surround it.

But perhaps the most important dimension of contemporary patterns of youthful alienation which the parties have not faced is the particularly powerful combination of economic stratification and exclusion with political disenfranchisement. The geographical concentration of areas of affluence and poverty has become even more marked and divisive since 1979, an outcome of the two nations strategy pursued by the Thatcher governments.[5] The category of 'youth' tells us little about the even more important differences of experience and life chances which divide young people. Their differing needs and interests rarely figure in public debate: where they do appear, young men are villains, joyriders and dealers, the wreakers of social havoc; whilst young women are allotted, amongst others, the roles of welfare scroungers and social victims. The realities are, of course, that young people live out a variety of different kinds of roles and lifestyle. Yet

5. Bob Jessop et al., *Thatcherism: a tale of two nations*, Polity Press, Cambridge 1988.

they find little connection between their daily struggles and the political debates they see and hear in the media and this is particularly true for the young jobless and low paid. Moreover, the young are figured as objects of a highly moralistic discourse from the political right, which has recently been echoed by some of New Labour's leading politicians.

The increasing gap between young people and official party politics is, however, only one manifestation of a set of fairly complicated changes which have disturbed the relationship between the political parties and civil society. It is not just young people whose loyalties have proved harder to command since the 1950s. The apparent disaffection of younger generations with official politics offers a highly concentrated and more dramatic example of these processes.

However, three caveats to the idea that young people have become irredeemably alienated from (official) politics should be registered. First, there is a large social science literature, especially in the US, devoted to the study of the changing attitudes of individuals across different generational phases of their lives. One important strand of interpretation suggests that younger people are always more cynical about politics than their elders, and that this attitude mellows with age. On this view, 'Generation X' is no different from its predecessors.[6]

Second, some commentators assert that new types of politics have absorbed the interests and energies of the younger generation, although this claim needs to be treated with some care. Whilst the participation of younger people in groups like Greenpeace, Amnesty International and a range of informal, direct action campaigns has undoubtedly proliferated in recent years, this 'new' politics remains the preserve of a tiny minority of young people in Britain. Perhaps most significantly of all in this context, the young have never constituted a coherent social interest which has mobilised as a social movement. Certainly, the new kinds of social movements which have sprung up since the 1960s have a particularly youthful inflection (though a generational gap between the new politics of the late 60s and those of the 1990s is now apparent). But the kinds of collective action in which young people have participated do not point in any single political direction. Moreover, it is simply not empirically true that movements with younger

6. M. Kent Jennings and Richard Niemi, *Generations and Politics*, Princeton University Press, Princeton 1981; and Sharon Warden, 'What's happened to youth attitudes since Woodstock?', *The Public Perspective*, 5, 1994, pp19-24.

participants are necessarily involved in a style which is more averse to conventional political lobbying than other organisations.

The third reason for scepticism about the simple picture of youth lack of interest in contemporary politics stems from the interesting, if still contentious, ideas of post-materialist theorists. This school, most commonly associated with the work of Ronald Ingelhart and his collaborators, argues that generational changes provide the key to some of the most salient cleavages in politics and social attitude which prevail today.[7] Locating a seismic shift in political values amongst the generation which grew up in the conditions of affluence of the 1950s and 60s, these commentators argue that the emergence of new types of issues on the political agendas of modern states is a direct result of this generation's concern for quality of life issues, now that their basic economic security had been guaranteed, as well as of the impact of movements like feminism on a wide range of young people. Issues connected with personal identity, lifestyle and morality are now supplanting the economic concerns that shaped the politics of earlier generational cohorts. Interestingly, Blair has at times presented his own politics in a similar way. Whilst debates continue about the empirical and theoretical viability of post-materialist analysis, it presents an interesting alternative perspective on the question of youth participation within the political system: if Ingelhart and his collaborators are right, then the gap between the interests and aspiration of younger people and the agendas of the political parties should close as post-materialist issues penetrate the political system.

Yet there are few grounds for optimism on this question. The enduring capacity of Britain's representative democracy to reproduce a political community which looks pretty homogenous in its ethnic, gender and age characteristics does not bode well. Some critics have pointed to the ritualised and socially conservative atmosphere which suffuses British parliamentary debate, making it seem remote and dull to an audience reared on a faster and slicker cultural style. But on the other hand, one might argue that the history of Western Europe is littered with examples of states reinventing their relationship with civil societies, devising new channels of communication, assimilating new social interests and overhauling their political agendas in response to increasingly disaffected outsider groups. Some of the problems outlined here may be unique to the British system,

---

7. Ronald Ingelhart, *The Silent Revolution*, Princeton University Press, Princeton 1977.

but others are not, suggesting that lessons may be gleaned from other states.

One brief example illustrates this. In the US, one way in which the more corrosive forms of individualisation within young people's lives have been countered is through the ethos and practice of community service. These have gone unremarked in Britain in the debates which have broken out about Etzioni's brand of communitarianism. Many high schools, colleges and universities in the US encourage, and some require, a commitment to service to other social groups. This involves students in a variety of services of benefit to their community. On many campuses these activities are voluntarily undertaken by student organisations and groups, to an extent which has no equivalent in Britain.

'Issues connected with quality of life are now supplanting the economic concerns that shaped the politics of earlier generations'

Critics see these activities as a poor antidote to the deeply entrenched economic inequalities which pervade American society. But the fact remains that many young people in the US are at an early stage invited to engage in community activities - working in disadvantaged schools, with disabled groups or the elderly for example - in a way that allows them to imagine a stronger sense of public good, some kind of antidote to the corrosive individualism and privatism of American life. One of the benefits of this kind of experience is that it at least allows a debate to begin about what community means, and what young people can give to and learn about other social groups; and it raises the social value of the participants. This is a far cry from the notion of deference to community values, or the increasingly fashionable moralistic response to social problems which stresses the individual's regulation of her own conduct in line with a fixed value system imposed from above. Thinking about communities as diverse, overlapping and essentially malleable entities should allow for discussion of how young people contribute to the wider public good and the lives of the communities in which they live. This is a very different undertaking from framing youth as a problem of social order which needs firmer policing: better, surely, to regard young people as actors engaged in particular kinds of struggle for their own forms of social and political identity, who find the paths to adult citizenship blocked, irrelevant or unappealing.

Re-establishing connections between young people and the political community remains an apparently intractable problem for modern states. Initiatives like Rock the Vote, or Blair's appeal to younger people to join the remodelled Labour Party, are important moves in this context, but unlikely to dismantle the obstacles to a wider pattern of participation within the political system. Debate needs to focus on which forms the political system might devise to secure channels between the state and the wider society, and how political debate can respond to the needs and interests of the different youth communities and interests. If 'New Labour' really means what it says - that it wants to recreate a vibrant civic life - then it must summon the same reforming zeal that it has hitherto focused solely upon the Labour Party and open up an agenda here. Young people's assemblies, a youth bill of rights, MP's surgeries for the young are the kinds of proposals that merit consideration. But more than any specific set of recommendations, the party needs to open a discussion that involves a wide range of public voices and interests, and addresses the connections between this issue and related questions about the apparent crises of adult identity and morality in contemporary Britain. Labour might begin here by abandoning the word 'youth' in its literature and addressing the various communities and interests lurking underneath an increasingly inappropriate label.

Thanks to Tom Porter for help with some of the information in this article.

Bypassing Politics?

The contradictions of 'DiY culture'

Peter Gartside

*Peter Gartside explores aspects of 'DiY Culture',
arguing for a critical engagement with, and
differentiation of, this loose 'movement'. Can we
'understand' this style of politics according to
existing notions of what constitutes 'radical' politics.*

For me, it seemed a symbolic moment. The anti-Criminal Justice Bill march/
rally, Hyde Park, October 1994. Some of us are respectfully listening to the
platform speakers - Labour dissidents, SWP, Liberty, Arthur Scargill - when we
become aware that behind us a rave party is getting under way. A sound-system
on the back of a truck has somehow made its way up Park Lane, pumping out
the soon to be criminalised 'repetitive beats'. For an instant there is a tension:
should we stay here - the speakers themselves are beginning to get repetitive -
or go and have a dance? As I like to remember it, significant numbers at that
moment literally turned their backs on the platform and went to join the 'DiY'
carnival. But although I like this as a metaphor, it is not because I want to suggest
there has been some final, radical shift in protest politics; the situation I want to
look at is more complex.

As anyone who has followed the political scene in the last few years will
know, an apparently new style of protest politics - what has come to be called
'DiY Culture' - has blossomed. A new generation of activists has bypassed

organised politics and ecological pressure groups, instead adopting imaginative Non Violent Direct Action (NVDA) tactics, most notably around anti-road protest. An informal network of activists and campaigns now exists with its own relatively sophisticated 'underground' media.[1] The solidarity between different campaigns has in a sense been cemented by their common opposition to, and victimisation by, the Criminal Justice and Public Order Act (1994). The CJA hit at, amongst other things, 'DiY'/ Rave culture, at 'new age' travellers and other alternative lifestyles, and at NVDA as a way of doing politics. Lumping together the different manifestations of this style of protest into some sort of 'new social movement' is problematic, however. The various protests are relatively structureless and - despite this often being characterised as 'single issue' politics - interact in complex ways. The emphasis is on creative action rather than 'theorising'. It can make for a confusing picture.

There is, of course, a danger of overstating the importance of Direct Action politics, of extrapolating from the amount of coverage these colourful and eminently photogenic protests have received. This kind of committed activism is a minority, and localised, pursuit among young people. It is a sign of our impoverished political culture that the protestors' committed, oppositional, outlaw aura has been seized on so keenly, indeed romanticised, by some commentators, notably in the pages of the *Guardian*. It is easy to eulogise these 'grassroots' protests uncritically, particularly when parliamentary politics seems, especially to young people, grey, media- and soundbite led and increasingly oblivious to everyday concerns. It is also clear that 'the left' as a focus for oppositional politics simply does not exist for many young people. The ideological convergence of the two main political parties has left many of us feeling unrepresented, angry and depressed. It warms the left-leaning, anti-Tory heart to see young people committed to *anything* other than individualism and consumption in these post-modern, post-collectivist New Times.

I don't want simply to turn this on its head and debunk DiY culture. But, as Mike Waite in *Soundings 3* insists, these protests deserve a critical scrutiny they haven't so far received, including some differentiation between different strands within the 'movement'. Important questions remain as to how to think about

---

1. The best example I have come across is *Squall* magazine, PO Box 8959, London N19 5HW. Any issue will include details of the main campaigning groups.

this style of politics, however. I think there is a tendency on the left to see environmental activism as analogous to those other 'new social movements' - feminism, black politics, gay and lesbian activism - and to try to co-opt it, somewhat opportunistically, to some sort of counterhegemonic project. Consequently, NVDA-style protest has been welcomed as a potentially reinvigorating force for the left. But this involves a questionable assumption that it shares goals or a political language with traditional left politics. The new protest groups have tended to be assessed from this perspective in terms of a 'radical' lineage of '(counter)cultures of resistance'. Measured in these terms it can quite easily be dismissed as inarticulate, disorganised, a re-hash of the woolliest aspects of hippy culture.

Probably like many others who set out to get involved with, and try to make sense of, NVDA/DiY culture, I have found it a sometimes frustrating experience. This is not simply because the diffuse nature of this activism - apparently disorganised (although it is worth saying that many of these protests are terrific, imaginative pieces of organisation), ad hoc, sometimes playful and anti-rational - makes it difficult to grasp what's going on. It is because this style of protest forces us to re-think the existing paradigms of what constitutes 'radical politics'. At 33, I'm old enough to dimly remember a Labour government, and although I have never been involved in organised politics, I grew up within a vaguely left-ish political culture of CND and Anti-Racism marches. For me, it is difficult to 'make sense' of this style of politics partly because the languages used by these protestors are not altogether commensurate with those of what I understand as 'left', or 'radical', politics. This is so for at least two reasons. Firstly NVDA protests represent, among other things, a critique of the rational, positivist languages of existing political culture, of which the marxist and socialist traditions are clearly a part; and, secondly, in a sense this is the politics of the Thatcher generation which has grown up during a period when the 'languages' of collectivism, unionism, even the idea of 'society', came under radical ideological attack. I would argue that to assume that this is a 'movement' which is, or should be, *necessarily* complementary to left politics - that what these protestors want is in some way the same as what 'we' want, did they but know it - or to think of it as just another 'new social movement', or to ignore, for example, its engagement with mysticism and holism, is to risk missing much of its contradictory richness.

The 'class politics' of nature

I find that the work of sociologist Klaus Eder provides a useful framework within which to think about some of the concerns of this new wave of protest.[2] Eder argues that a counterculture has always been present within modernity, but that it has recently been foregrounded by growing awareness of what he calls 'the ecological crisis'. He suggests that what has distinguished this counterculture from the dominant strand of modernism, whether capitalist or marxist, has been its radically different relationship with nature. Broadly, Eder's thesis is that the class politics of modernity have been fought on the shared assumption that nature is at the service of 'man'. The key struggle has hitherto been over ownership of the means of production, while it is the counterculture which has sustained a critique of the discourse of industrial and scientific progress. The situation, in Eder's account, has become more urgent with the growing realisation of 'the self-defeating process of modernisation'(p119). While even technocrats now speak a softened green language of environmental concern, this crisis has provided countercultural factions with their opportunity for historical action. Eder writes mostly from the German experience, but in an English context historical manifestations of this counterculture might include Romanticism, the pastoral, utopian socialist tradition of William Morris, the Edwardian 'back to the land' ethic of Edward Carpenter and his fellow New Lifers, as well as the more recent manifestations - the 'Free Festivals and Fairs of Albion' - charted by George McKay in his book *Senseless Acts of Beauty*.[3] It is important to note, however, that this nature-loving, anti-rationalist, anti-modernist counterculture is politically ambivalent; it transcends the left-right political divide precisely because of this critical orientation towards 'progress' or modernity. Eder's conception of the counterculture would include aristocratic and anti-democratic currents and conservationist 'heritage' discourses as well as hippy/punk anarchist communes of the type McKay sees as antecedents of the new wave of DiY Culture and Direct Action politics.

Eder conceptualises a whole new 'class' struggle focused on the cultural field of 'Nature'. The countercultural relationship with nature - holistic and harmonious, even 'moral' - is pitted against the technocrats' and modernisers' instrumental and

---

2. *The New Politics of Class: Social Movements and Cultural Dynamics in Advanced Societies*, Sage, London 1993.
3. Verso, London 1996.

exploitative one. The middle classes are the main protagonists because, in his view, they are the class who feel most affronted by the effects of industrialism, pollution, etc. But Eder also acknowledges that in practice the counterculture can become a backward-looking 'bourgeois fugitive movement', tending to want to wish modernity away. His analysis is a bit schematic and overly developmental: he seems to suggest that this politics mobilised around nature and the 'good life' will supersede politics based on distributive justice, just as that superseded a politics based on political emancipation. The merit of the analysis, however, is that it raises the question of the class constitution and political orientation of a more rigorous conception of a 'counterculture', and that it allows us to conceive of such a 'movement' as 'radical' in a different way, in a different language, and to different ends from those of the dominant tradition of political and cultural critique, marxism.

Even though I find Eder's a useful framework for looking at possible post-industrial collectivities and solidarities beyond those of traditional left politics, I feel that the new environmental protest politics can only partly be accounted for in Eder's terms. It is certainly true that 'Nature' is an important, positive term in much of Direct Action politics - although it is also important to say that the anthropomorphic 'Nature' that is valued for its authenticity in the discourse of 'Mother Earth' is thoroughly constructed and, of course, gendered. Aspects of the anti-road protests at Newbury and Twyford Down do strike me as understandable in Eder's terms: as utopian, as an escapist 'bourgeois fugitive movement', *and* as an important critique of hegemonic rationalist modernity. And whether the kind of protests I am constructing as a movement are dominated by 'middle class' young people is a moot point. From an orthodox left political point of view it would be tempting to be dismissive of the new protest as the romanticism of a post-scarcity middle class. In this sense its 'radical' credentials depend on it being a protest of the marginalised, the excluded, rather than of voluntary 'drop-outs'. I think DiY Culture actually comprises an uneasy and problematic alliance of the two. Self-mythologising rhetoric about 'displaced commoners' and adoption of the seventeenth century Diggers as model 'radicals' seems like bourgeois romanticism to me, part of 'The Good Life' tradition of middle class 'voluntary simplicity'. But these protests also include, at the other extreme, people who have borne the brunt of the New Right onslaught on the welfare state: jobless, homeless and without adequate state benefits or a registered vote. Certainly the Wandsworth 'Pure Genius' land occupation, initially organised by 'The Land is Ours' campaign group, seemed to struggle to reconcile these contradictory elements. My impression of it was of just such a combination of idealists for whom it was an experimental, utopian eco-village, pragmatists interested in bringing about planning policy changes via the orthodox political channels and those in between; but it also became a place for London's destitute and the mentally ill to wash up. The *Guardian*'s John Vidal and George Monbiot, two of the key mainstream media proponents of Direct Action politics, rather puzzlingly characterised these problems as culminating in 'anarchy', which presumably might have been the point for some of the occupants.

Mystic-holism

I find it difficult to surmount my prejudice against the mystic-holistic rhetoric in which the defence of Nature in anti-road protest has often been couched. Much has been written recently about an apparent upsurge in anti-rational (or irrational) beliefs: esoteric religions, paganism, astrology, Tarot, *The X-files* and the 'unexplained'. It is a cultural phenomenon that deserves scrutiny beyond the lazy assumption that it is pre-millennium tension, or the latest recurrence of *fin-de-siecle-ism*. Mike Waite is right to want to take seriously the espousal of mysticism and paganism 'the re-invention of ancient rituals and interest in 'magick' of the Stanworth protestors, rather than to join in 'dismissive rationalist contempt'. The problem is how to approach positively this intrinsic feature of the new activism. It is clearly connected to that general valorisation of Nature and the natural already noted. And, being charitable, it can be read as an attempt to re-enchant everyday life, as a postmodern nostalgia for authenticity and community and something to believe in, as an expression of aspects of social desire not catered for in our individuated and commodified culture, or by politics as it is currently practised. I think it is important to recognise the subjective needs this activism and romanticism meet. It is too easy to adopt a judgemental, instrumental stance which denies the immediate pleasures of direct activism.

I find 'new-ageism' problematic only to the extent that the veneration of all things 'authentically' ancient, mythical and mystical - Celtic, Arthurian, Druidic or whatever - can tip over into a pernicious nationalism. This sort of mystical sense of belonging has been a feature of high profile anti-road protests which were mobilised around a desire to save the English countryside, at Twyford Down and Newbury in particular. The veneration of 'our' imperilled countryside is a regressive, but deep-rooted part of English culture. Anti-modernism and anti-urbanism have a long cultural history, some of which has been bound up with an insidious discourse of ethnic purity, a tradition of 'the re-invention of tradition' which is not merely quaint or eccentric.[4] Where the mysticism taps into national myths around 'the

'The veneration of all things "authentically" ancient can tip over into pernicious nationalism'

land' a critique can be mounted on the basis that historically this mixture of romanticism and ecologism, of nature and the land has been mobilised by the far right in a racist, *'volk-ish'* discourse. This is not to say that the Newbury or Twyford anti-roads protestors or land rights campaigners have propounded ethnic exclusivity

or ever would. It would be wrong to interpret the fact that these protests are overwhelmingly made up of white people as a consequence of active exclusion. It is, however, possible that the 'unlikely alliances' with middle England and the rural squirearchy in which these two protests found themselves might have been eased by the uncritical way hegemonic ideas about an idealised English countryside were deployed. It is also possible to think of this strange youthful invocation of nation (young Britain meets Old England) - contemporaneous, incidentally, with the monocultural idea of Britpop and Blair's 'New Britain' vision of a 'young country' - as a complex and confused response to unsettling forces of globalisation and cultural fragmentation: a longing for belonging, for a comforting sense of rootedness and authenticity.

We might also see current cultural trends towards anti-rationalism as real historical confirmation of the postmodernist insistence that instrumental rationality or 'the Enlightenment project' has run out of ideological steam. Is anti-rationalism the return of modernity's repressed, and might it therefore hold a positive potential for liberation? If postmodernists critique modernity for the regulative violence its binary epistemological structures do, should we not celebrate the outbreak of un-reason, alternative epistemologies and 'performative' physicality (raving, neo-pagan tattooing and piercing, and dressing up)? Dipping into pagan animism and the like is part of the playfulness of this style of protest and is perhaps more parodic than anything. This is also

---

4. Patrick Wright has written extensively on unsavoury connections between 'blood and soil' in his *On Living in an Old Country*, Verso, London 1985, and *The Village that Died for England*, Jonathan Cape, London 1995.

an aspect of the *bricolage* of styles and tribal motifs - North American Indian, Aboriginal, Celtic - widely adopted in this protest culture. For me, the playfulness and imagination of the new protest movement is one of its charms, a sense of fun which ought to be taken seriously, as it were. It is my feeling, for example, that the untogether amateurishness for which Mike Waite criticises the Stanworth protest can be read positively as a self-conscious refusal of mainstream careerist, professional politics. There is a lot that is carnivalesque in the new protest. Such playfulness is often adopted as an affront to the 'straight world'; dressing up in a rabbit costume or as a pantomime horse to play cat and mouse with the security men in the Newbury woods makes the police look silly when they try to arrest you. Adopting quasi-pagan rituals might be as much a form of parody as wearing a fluorescent uniform emblazoned with 'POLITE' rather than 'POLICE'.

In the cities

One of the ways I would internally differentiate this loose movement is between those protests which have been mobilised in defence of Mother Earth/the English countryside, and those which engage with more difficult, complex, urban everyday issues: the protests against the M11 at 'Wanstonia', Reclaim the Streets, Critical Mass cycling actions and the Wandsworth 'Pure Genius' land occupation, campaigns which are anti-'car culture' but also *for* community involvement in planning, housing and so on. Given that most of us live in cities and might continue to want to do so, these campaigns are addressing vital and potentially mainstream issues.

The increasing privatisation and individualisation of everyday life has been a depressing feature of recent times (which is not, incidentally, to suggest some *Coronation Street* golden age of community). There seems to be a widespread fear and loathing of cities in contemporary culture, fear of crime and for personal safety (despite the reassurances of statistical evidence) and anxiety about traffic and pollution. The Tory - and, sadly, New Labour - response to 'crime' and 'anti-social behaviour' has been increasingly authoritarian and regulatory. The penetration of CCTV and private security into increasingly privatised civic spaces, for example, has gone largely unopposed. At the same time we have been treated to a tide of rhetoric about the need to re-establish the idea of 'community'. I am not sure how this could be possible in cities in which the use of space is determined by developers, which are choked with traffic and regulated in the interest of that ambiguous notion 'security'. Campaigns which challenge the uses of urban space ('Pure Genius' was amongst other things about the way planning law works against the creative, community-based, human-needs use of often derelict city space; Reclaim the Streets is about making streets pleasant and communal places to *be in*, rather than efficient or scary conduits to rush along) have done so by actually creating spaces to show what is possible. Reclaim the Streets actions - literally occupying streets and blocking traffic - have raised such issues by creating, however temporarily, an imaginative, alternative vision of public spaces; physical human spaces and open, discursive spaces in which meanings can be made without predetermined agendas. In so doing they have mounted an important critique of those processes of individualisation, privatisation and regulation which have made cities depressing places to live.

When Reclaim the Streets - which, for an afternoon, was a 'campaign group' of thousands of people - took over the M41 in west London (in a breathtaking feat of organisation) it/they/we created a space in which it seemed anything could happen. This wasn't a 'festival' or a 'rave' in the organised, policed and commodified sense - although the sound systems provided an optional focus to the event - nor was it a 'protest march' in the orthodox sense. There was no platform, no speeches, no leaders, no formalised statement of demands. The action created something like what the self-styled 'ontological anarchist' Hakim Bey calls a 'Temporary Autonomous Zone', a window of creative possibility.[5] This 'DiY' ethic has nothing to do with 'self-help' individualism but is both a form of collectivism and an expression of resistance to our commodified culture. For example, the strands of rave culture with which the movement is entwined are self-consciously opposed to the commodification of ecstasy/dance culture exemplified by the superclubs (Ministry of Sound, Cream, etc) and licensed mega-raves like Tribal Gathering. It is making your own fun, rather than buying into it, which is important.

Political debate, like an active sense of community, requires public spaces, channels of communication. The fragmentation of the public sphere - a direct consequence of New Right policies - and the resultant impoverishment of 'politics', mean that efforts like Reclaim the Streets can produce only a contingent

5. *T.A.Z. The Temporary Autonomous Zone, Ontological Anarchy, Poetic Terrorism*, Autonomedia, New York 1991.

and temporary collectivism, even though people take away an inspiration and a sense of meaning which outlasts the moment. It does, however, mean that we can't talk about this 'movement' - if it is one - in terms of a coherent grouping based on some objective class community of interest. And this is where we need to be wary of quasi-Gramscian talk of alliance building and so on. The problem with any attempt to build a counterhegemony is precisely the seemingly irreversible fragmentation of the traditional forms of collectivist political culture. There are positive things to be said for the freeing up of old rigidities: a weakening of deference and of prescribed gender roles, for example. But the danger of this fragmentation is that we are left in a situation in which political cultures with different and possibly incommensurate visions have no common arena - a public sphere - in which they can talk.

It also needs to be acknowledged that this 'movement' enjoys its underground, anti-authority status. There is a degree of self-conscious rebelliousness in these protests which works against the possibilities for forming wider alliances with the 'straight world' of progressive/left politics. In the sense that DiY Culture has been formed by its marginalisation in the unfriendly circumstances it grew up in, it will always be resistant to assimilation. I am not sure that a certain symbiosis doesn't exist between DiY culture's romantic countercultural stance, and the dominant political culture. In any event, I doubt that New Labour's vision of an inclusive society: family oriented, stakeholding and responsible, a somewhat conformist christian liberal utopia, would include space for DiY Culture. Similarly, this type of protest has an ambivalent relationship with the (official) media. While many of the protests seem designed to be as outrageous and spectacular as possible, they are also resistant to, or bitter about, the media-isation of their politics. The problem, of course, given that the idea of 'politics' now seems constituted by what happens in the media, is that in pursuing politics outside orthodox media channels this becomes protest in a vacuum, leaving the structures of power unmolested. Either protest politics and Westminster may simply remain indifferent to each other, or we will see more of the same authoritarian, pathologising response to the emergence of collective protest based on new, contingent solidarities.

To generalise from my own partial experience, I find the utopian 'back to the land' aspects of this contradictory protest culture somewhat sentimental and wilfully simplistic. It's easy to understand, and to feel, the attraction of abstractions like simplicity or 'nature', and presumably most people can support, to some extent, the preservationist impulse. But the need is to find ways of living together and belonging not based on nation, or 'tradition' or 'golden age' notions of rural arcadia. This is not to say that anti-bypass protest is a soft option, or that it hasn't been valuable in highlighting transport policy as an important instance of free-market madness, or revealing just how deeply the Tory attack on civil liberties runs. It's probably clear that what fires my imagination more are those campaigns based around a desire to make cities better places to live in. Reclaim the Streets's anonymous pamphleteers have made connections beyond the simple anti-'car culture' issue - 'The streets are as full of capitalism as of cars and the pollution of capitalism is much more insidious' - while also insisting on the political nature of the carnival, and the importance of a pluralist, open city.

Although I remain ambivalent, DiY Culture has, for me, already made a contribution towards a less narrow, authoritarian and centralised conception of political culture, a proper engagement with environmental concerns (and not just of a conservationist type), and has energised new forms of collective action and solidarity which respect difference in lifestyles and beliefs. Finally, I can't be alone in finding myself lost for somewhere to take my feelings of disenchantment, still in a position somewhere between the languages of old/New left politics and the utopian thrill of 'DiY Culture', and, as I was in Hyde Park, feeling the pull of, while ambivalent about, both. An interesting place to be.